Tug-O War
A FLY-FISHER'S GAME

Nick Curcione

Capt. Joe Blados Illustrations

Tug-O-War
A FLY-FISHER'S GAME

Nick Curcione

Frank Amato

PORTLAND

To my wife Kathy and
all my fishing friends.

Frank Amato Publications, Inc.
P.O. Box 82112, Portland, Oregon 97282
503•653•8108 • www.amatobooks.com

All photographs by Nick Curcione unless otherwise noted.
Illustrations: Capt. Joe Blados
Knot Illustrations: Kevin Sedlak
Book & Cover Design: Kathy Johnson
Printed in Hong Kong

Softbound ISBN: 1-57188-250-2   UPC: 0-66066-00439-0
Hardbound ISBN: 1-57188-263-4   UPC: 0-66066-00452-9

1 3 5 7 9 10 8 6 4 2

Contents

Introduction

I'm sure all of you are familiar with the expression that tells us wisdom comes with age. Of course, all you have to do is look around to find plenty of evidence to the contrary. But like many beliefs that have been passed down through the ages, there is a kernel of truth in this observation. For myself at least, and most of my buddies, it has certainly applied to our fishing experiences. Practically all my fishing savvy is the result of what I have learned from a lifetime of fishing with close friends. And now as I reflect on it, I realize that this sharing of knowledge and experience is one of the qualities that continues to kindle my love for this sport.

In terms of angling effectiveness, the fishing knowledge I've managed to accumulate significantly enhances my time on the water. As in any sport, there's an immense degree of satisfaction that accrues with mastery of the fundamentals. Learning how to use your tackle, reading the water for telltale signs otherwise hidden from the untrained eye, skillfully subduing your quarry and returning it to its watery realm so it has the chance to challenge us another day; these are tremendous pleasures in their own right. However, the most meaningful feature of my fishing career goes way beyond my accomplishments as an angler. Instead, it has to do with the enduring friendships that have developed over the years.

In my younger days when I was a regular on the Southern California party boat circuit I met an older gent who told me that he never got skunked when he went fishing. Judging by the fish he consistently brought aboard, it was obvious he knew what he was doing, but taking his statement literally, I was skeptical that he always caught fish every time he went out. Apparently he read the expression of disbelief on my face and went on to explain that by not getting skunked he meant that he always managed to have a good time on the water regardless of how poor the fishing might be. I still looked puzzled and the old guy proceeded to give me my first direct lesson on the meaning of friendship. Whenever possible he made it a practice to go fishing with at least one friend and for him, that was the high point of the outing. He loved to catch fish as much as anyone, but he wasn't about to let the changing moods of Mother Nature intrude on the quality time he was spending with his friends.

Like the good Dr. Freud was fond of saying, there is understanding and there is understanding. The old gent spoke in plain English and I understood what he said, but at the time, I really didn't have a deep appreciation for the message he was trying to convey. I had my fishing buddies and I loved being with them, but the primary focus in those early days was catching fish and if we didn't fare well, we didn't think we had a good trip. It took some time, but

The author and Captain Paul Dixon with a Key Largo permit.

gradually I began to learn what the old boy was talking about. The fishing experience entails a lot more than simply pursuing and catching fish. Even for those times when you can't get out on the water, the friendships and camaraderie remain.

Today, the most precious dividends I derive from the world of sport fishing are the close bonds that I have with others who share the same passion. These relationships have significantly enhanced my life both on and off the water. I never stop learning about the seemingly endless facets of this sport, and the added bonus is that most of this learning process takes place in the context of valued friendships. It is this dual quality of the fly-fishing experience, learning by having a great time with others, that I hope I can convey to you the reader.

CHAPTER 1

Tackling the Equipment Issue: Fly Rods and Reels

Sitting in the skiff watching my guide swing the baited end of the hand line above his head in circles that looked as uniform as a hula hoop, brought back memories of the rodeo ropers I used to see as a kid. It also felt a little strange to suddenly switch roles. After two days of giving casting instruction at a fly-fishing outing I was hosting in Mexico's Ascension Bay, it was my turn to be the student once again. Tomas, who had so convincingly demonstrated his expertise with the push pole, giving me repeated shots at wary schools of bonefish, was now trying to teach me the art of throwing a hand line. My high-tech fly outfit, which looked almost surrealistic propped against the background of the rough-hewn skiff, seemed strangely out of place. I have about $1200 worth of tackle sitting alongside me and I'm fishing with a hand line and spark plug sinker combination that probably wouldn't set you back more than three bucks. So why do this? The answer is simple, because it's a lot of fun, because it brought back childhood memories when all I had to fish with was a hand line. I never lost the thrill of the sensation that is telegraphed to your fingers and hands when a fish hits and the line suddenly comes tight. That is why I love to fly-fish. Because the line is manipulated directly by hand, you have instant communication with the fish.

My first rod-and-reel combination was a bait-casting outfit and when spinning gear became more readily available, I fished both types of tackle. Each system had their unique advantages and shortcomings but for many years they were all I fished with and I had a lot of fun. Yet, something was missing, and it wasn't until I started fly-fishing over 30 years ago, that I re-captured the unique sensation I used to experience when I fished with hand lines.

Notwithstanding Tomas's skill in throwing the hand line, the one major difference in using fly tackle is that

Master angler Stu Apte with a yellowfin taken aboard the Royal Star.

In contests with strong, saltwater game fish, fly reels become an integral part of the fish-fighting process.

you cast the line with a rod. Why use a rod? Because it is more efficient than a simple hand line. You can throw a nearly weightless fly much further and with a lot more accuracy than would be possible with the hand line alone. In conjunction with the reel that holds the line, the rod also helps you fight the fish. Whether or not these additional elements provide more enjoyment than a simple hand line is a subjective judgment that you must make yourself. At least with today's advanced manufacturing technology, you have the option of making a lot of choices in terms of how you want to fish.

Today's fly-tackle industry is about as good an example as any of the free-enterprise principle that extols the virtues of open-market competition. The present generation of fly-fishers has an unprecedented choice of high-quality gear designed explicitly for use in salt water. A mere 20 years ago this segment of the industry was still in its infancy. Most fly-fishing manufacturers simply did not think in terms of saltwater tackle because there was so little demand for it. Consequently, those who wanted to venture forth in the salt had a very limited range of tackle selection. If you wanted a high-quality reel that would stand up to the challenges of hard pulling, and oftentimes comparatively large game fish, your choice was virtually narrowed to either a Fin-Nor or Seamaster. How times have changed! At a recent fly-tackle exposition, a friend told me he counted over 60 reel manufacturers, almost all of whom have models aimed at the saltwater market.

Also gone are the days when so-called saltwater fly rods were little more than beefed-up versions of their freshwater counterparts. I still have an old 11-weight fiberglass stick that has the tiny stripper and snake guides normally found on trout rods. An 11-weight floating line barely squeezes through. If a knot or line tangle develops, you're in trouble. The manufacturer may have legitimately intended the rod for the salt, but the design philosophy was still in the freshwater realm. Fortunately, that is no longer the case and there are at least a dozen major companies manufacturing top-quality rods that are designed specifically to meet the demands of fly-fishing in salt water.

Saltwater Fly Rods

Because it is the most critical component in the fly-tackle system, let us take a look at rods first. Compared to the mechanical complexity of reels, most rods seem like an object lesson in simplicity. But particularly where fly rods are concerned, appearances can be deceiving. The first consideration to bear in mind is that it is the rod, not the reel, that is the principal fish-fighting tool. The old commercial fishing practice known as "jack poling," where fish were literally plucked from the sea by pulling on them with long Calcutta poles, illustrates this point dramatically. No reels were needed. The barbless, feathered jig was presented to the fish (primarily tuna that were drawn to the surface with live chum) by manipulating the pole in sort of a figure-eight pattern. When the fish hit the jig, the pole was put to the ultimate test. It had to withstand the tremendous opposing forces of the tuna trying to gain its freedom and the fisherman leaning back attempting to lift it

*The right tackle coupled with the services of an experienced guide like
Dan Marini can make for a very productive outing.*

onboard. The pole also had to have the ability to flex otherwise the fisherman might suddenly find himself swimming with a school of frenzied tuna.

Whenever I was asked to make recommendations for rods suitable for big-game, long-range fishing, I would refer to the jack pole as a point of reference. With the exception of its length, it was the ideal big-game rod. In this type of fishing, the sole purpose of the rod is to subdue fish. Casting is not a consideration. With the jack pole the feathered jig was simply dropped into the water. The procedure is practically the same when using conventional tackle big-game outfits. In many cases the bait or trolling lure is dropped over the side of the boat. Even on long-range boats where anglers often chuck large baits with big-game outfits, the rod's casting characteristics are irrelevant. The distance involved is minimal, usually only a few yards out away from the boat. Besides, since the bait can easily tear loose from the hook, a distance-enhancing speed-up-and-stop-casting motion is out of the question. You could probably effect the same sort of easy lob cast with a broom stick. Thus comparatively speaking, big-game rod design is not all that complicated. The rod has to have tremendous lifting power coupled with a flex pattern that places minimal stress on the angler, and that's about it. I do recall

however, an overzealous, obviously uninformed sales person extolling the sensitivity virtues of a blue-water rod he was trying to sell to a fellow who was going to make his first long-range trip. I felt compelled to interrupt and the first chance I had to talk to the customer away from the salesman, I told him that the sensitivity factor in a rod like this was pure bogus. In big-game fishing, if you cannot detect the sensation when a billfish or tuna takes a bait or strikes a trolling lure, you have some serious neurological problems and shouldn't be fishing in the first place.

However, unlike conventional big-game rods, fly rods pose a more difficult design problem. Particularly where saltwater species are involved, the rod must have the muscle to handle powerful fish. But it must also exhibit excellent casting characteristics. Fly-casting is an integral part of fly-fishing and the rod is the key component in the delivery system. Not long ago this point was driven home to a friend of mine, Jim Skydel, a recognized surgeon with excellent eye-hand coordination (a comforting thought if you ever need his services). Given his physical ability, I was a little puzzled when he told me about the difficulty he was having in trying to throw a tight straight line. We met at a casting pond near his home where he proudly displayed a custom-built 6-weight rod that he recently purchased from a local rod maker. I told him to make a few casts, and while his strokes looked good, I had to agree with him about the line's broken profile. Half jokingly I told him that it had more waves in it than a group of grandparents saying good-bye at an airport. I asked to make a few casts with the rod and didn't fare much better. This was one of those instances where the rod was at fault not the caster. I don't know who the blank manufacturer was, but the rod vibrated like a car antenna being struck by a tree branch. I told him to give the rod to someone he didn't like.

Over the years I have served as a consultant for various rod companies spanning the entire range of tackle modes, conventional, spinning and fly. They are all recognized companies manufacturing quality products and while I'm no engineer, using all these different sticks has certainly enhanced my ability to determine when a rod fishes and casts well. In 1997 I had the privilege of joining the Thomas and Thomas advisory staff and without question this has given me the opportunity to fish some of the best rods available anywhere at any price. Today there are only a handful of truly talented rod designers and Tom Dorsey, who originally founded the company, ranks among the very best. If you were looking for the embodiment of a Renaissance Man, Tom is certainly it. He's an accomplished jazz bassist, an expert carpenter, has a masters in philosophy and was going to pursue the Ph.D. only to get sidetracked by his passion for building fly rods. If you could get your hands on one, his early split cane rods are true collector pieces. When you combine his innate talent with his perfectionist personality, it's easy to see why every rod that leaves the factory is first-rate. In fairness, of course, there are a number of other major manufacturers such as Sage, Scott and Powell to name a few, who also offer top-quality rods. From time to time I fish their rods and I know from first-hand experience that if you purchase one of their models you can be assured that it will incorporate all the necessary features for this type of fishing. The other consideration to bear in mind is that the quality of the rod notwithstanding, the primary factor that makes for good casting is plain old practice. It's really the same story with most pieces of equipment we own, from cameras to computers and cars. They tend to be far more capable than the people using them. As Lefty Kreh is fond of saying, any rod that will set you back more than a couple of hundred bucks will cast better than about 95% of the people using them. So if you are not casting as well as you think you should be (and this is probably a

well-founded self-criticism) buying a more expensive rod most likely will not result in any measurable improvement. Competent instruction and constant practice are the paths to casting excellence.

In terms of materials, the company I work with makes some of the world's finest split cane rods, a craft where Tom Dorsey is truly a master. But these are not what you want for saltwater fishing. Split cane does not hold up well when subjected to the ravages of salt water. It would sort of be like off-roading in Baja with a Rolls Royce. In addition, the very slow, progressive action which is the hallmark of these rods does not make for peak efficiency in terms of either the fish-fighting ability or casting effectiveness that is called for in a saltwater environment. Instead, graphite composites have proven far superior for rods designed for saltwater use. This material is generally incorporated into a taper design that can vary from moderate to fast. The taper in large part determines rod action or how the rod will bend. Split cane rods have mostly parabolic actions. Under pressure, the rod takes a deep bend along its entire section right down to the butt. This really isn't desirable for most saltwater situations where you have to lift fairly sizable fish up out of the depths. In the saltwater realm you

Fly rods can sometimes break at very inopportune times.

want a rod with a stiffer butt section that has the backbone to pressure powerful fish. Secondly, the rod should have the kind of action that affords maximum casting distance with almost effortless efficiency.

There are anglers who prefer slower-action rods and Thomas and Thomas, as do other manufacturers, offers models with fuller flexing patterns. To be honest, when I first cast some of these rods, I wasn't particularly fond of

The rod is the key component in the delivery system.

them, but after fishing some of the slower-action rods in the Horizon SC series, I came to appreciate the controlled flex action, especially when casting large poppers on weight-forward floating lines. However, for sinking lines and shooting heads (I'll have more to say about these lines in the next chapter) I prefer a faster tip action like you'll find on the standard Horizon series and the new Vectors. I really don't know how Tom managed it, but the Vector series with their incredible low swing weight and fast progressive action are some of the finest rods I have ever cast. Every good caster I know who has thrown a line with these rods has come away impressed. But this is not to say that you will favor every rod in the lineup. Even among accomplished casters, there are differences in style and this translates into different preferences. That is why all the manufacturers offer rods with a variety of actions. Therefore, my best advice is never buy a rod merely on someone else's recommendation. Before you lay out the bucks, cast it. Just about any established fly shop will have rods for you to cast and you should try out different rods from different manufacturers. Merely because you're absolutely in love with a certain company's 8-weight, doesn't mean that you'll feel the same way about their 10-weight and this holds true regardless of the manufacturer.

When you purchase a top-of-the-line rod from an established manufacturer, you can be assured that the guides, cork handles and reel seats will all be premium grade. One very important feature that you should look for is the size of the guides and tip top. During the cast, line does not shoot straight through the guides like a dart passing through a blowgun. It spirals which means that guides with small diameters will restrict line flow.

This impedes casting distance and any larger-diameter knots will cause problems akin to backups in your plumbing system. The crucial guide in this respect is the first guide up from the rod handle. It's referred to as the stripping or butt guide. At a minimum, the diameter of this guide should be at least 16 millimeters. Cosmetically it doesn't look as good, but on a number of my rods, even those as small as 6-weights, I've had the standard stripping guide replaced with one that is 20 millimeters in diameter. The effect is something like a volleyball going through a basketball hoop. There is much less restriction and you'll make longer casts.

When people talk about fly rods, two items you seldom hear mentioned are reel seats and rod grips, but these are important components you don't want to neglect when you're in the market for a new rod. As with other top-quality rods, Thomas and Thomas reel seats are machined anodized aluminum and on the saltwater rods, the two rings tighten in an up locking configuration moving away from the rod butt. This adds to the butt extension enabling you to rest the rod against your stomach when fighting a fish without having the reel brush against your body. It's important to have a seat that will hold the reel firmly in place. But you don't want one where you'll need vise grips to free the reel after only a few hours exposure to salt water. With good-quality reel seats, you shouldn't have any of these problems. The butt extension, or fighting butt as it is more commonly referred to, should not be more than about 2 inches in length otherwise you stand a good chance of snagging the fly line. The end portion should be rounded for optimum comfort. Some early-generation rods had fighting butts that could be likened to medieval torture instruments. After a day's fishing your midsection felt like it was pummeled by a jousting pole.

Apparently the one area where manufacturers must compromise is the design of the rod grip. The most popular configuration on saltwater rods is the Half and Full Wells design. Both of these feature a depression at the top portion of the grip where the thumb is pressed during the casting stroke. I prefer a more radical indentation on the forward and rear portion of the grip. Aside from the issue of appearance, manufacturers are reluctant to drastically alter rod-grip shapes because they receive conflicting demands from their customers. Some want large, almost baseball-like grips, while others prefer deep-scooped indentations. My friend John Napoli, a long-time member of the Long Beach Casting Club and a recognized tournament caster in his own right, convinced me that the radical Full Well design makes for more comfortable and efficient casting. I discussed this in my book on Baja and I think it bears repeating here.

According to Ed Jaworowski, another accomplished caster, the thumb functions like a rudder giving directional control as well as helping provide a secure grip on the rod. Proper casting form consists of a smoothly executed acceleration of the rod followed by a sudden stop. The thumb is critical in achieving this motion and to help it do its job, the grip should be shaped accordingly. If you are building a rod or want to modify the grip on one you have purchased, here is how to proceed. You will need an electric motor with a chuck to secure the end of the rod butt. A wood lathe is ideal, but regardless of how you go about this, it's important that the rod turn true otherwise you won't get a uniform contour.

Start with 80-grit sandpaper cut into strips about one inch wide and eight inches long. Grasp the sandpaper

Louisiana redfish.

strip by the ends and lay it roughly perpendicular to the cork grip. Be careful and use only light pressure on the sandpaper. Once you have begun to reduce the overall diameter of the grip, change to 150-grit sandpaper to begin the shaping phase. Periodically stop sanding and grasp the handle to see how it feels. Your hand should comfortably cradle the grip with the thumb resting naturally in the top indentation. Once the desired shape has been achieved, complete the sanding operation by going over the handle a few times with number 600 crocus cloth. This will yield a nice smooth finish.

Alright, assuming you are confident the rod has all "the right stuff" the remaining considerations are the rod's length, the number of sections and the weight of the fly line it will cast. Unlike the case with conventional and spinning rods, the choice of fly-rod length is somewhat limited. Both tradition and function have dictated that the most popular length, for saltwater rods at least, is nine feet. I suggest that unless you plan to use the rod on wide rivers where considerable line mending is necessary, do not opt for rods longer than nine feet. A few anglers are using the long salmon Spey rods in salt water, primarily in surf-fishing applications, where the added casting distance can be a definite advantage. They're also a lot of fun to use. Be advised however that their added length make for a poor fish-fighting tool. When pulling on a fish, the rod acts as a lever and the area on the rod grip above the reel where you do your lifting is the fulcrum. What this amounts to is a see-saw principle. As any child who has ever played on one knows, when the length of the board increases on one side of the fulcrum, the person on the long end gains a weight advantage and falls to the ground. It's the same when pulling on a fish with a rod. Here, the fish has the advantage because it is pulling on the long end of the rod. It stands to reason then, that as the rod is shortened, less advantage accrues to the fish. That is why some of the fly rods designed for big-game, blue-water fishing are shortened a bit to eight and a half feet.

Up until a few years ago most fiberglass and graphite fly rods were two-piece. Today manufacturers offer a wide choice of three- and four-piece models. What should you choose? Here the choice is quite simple. If you plan to use the rod exclusively in local waters where the only travel is by car, opt for a two-piece model. They are less expensive because the manufacturing process is simplified. However, if you plan on plane-trip destinations and want the security of carrying rods onboard with you, the multi-piece ones are the way to go. In case you are wondering, when you have a top-name-brand rod, the casting characteristics of two-piece and multi-piece models are virtually identical.

The question of what rod weight to buy is a bit more involved because a number of interrelated factors must be taken into account. Rod choice here is governed by the weight of the fly line you plan to use. This in turn is a function of the species you are targeting, the type of flies you'll be using and the conditions under which you are fishing. A good example here is yellowtail fishing in Southern California and Baja. Yellowtail are the kind of fish that like to pull you into bad places. They are primarily an inshore fish and frequent areas like rock pinnacles, reefs and kelp beds. If a section of kelp breaks loose and drifts offshore (referred to as a kelp paddy), it can serve as a haven for small baitfish which often attract yellowtail as well as other large predator game fish. Here you have the same fish, but under a very different set of conditions. Contrary to what some might expect, the yellows will

A 9-weight rod might be fine for the offshore paddy, but an 11-weight is more practical for the inshore work.

Striper fishing in the Northeast is another good example of the importance of different rods for the same fish under different sets of circumstance. In late spring there are a lot of salt ponds, estuaries and bays where you can experience some terrific action with stripers feeding on sand eels. A 2-inch Clouser Minnow tied on a 1/0 hook can make for a very convincing imitation. In these sheltered, relatively shallow waters, the fly doesn't need to be heavily weighted and you can have a ball with 7- and 8-weight rods. Weeks later if these fish move out to the rips to feed on squid, you'll need larger, weighted flies to draw their attention. Trying to throw a 5-inch pattern like a Popovics Shady Lady Squid with an 8-weight rod is going to entail a lot more effort and will be considerably less effective than would be the case if you switched to a 9- or 10-weight.

The author and his guide Suerdo releasing a tarpon at Casa Mar.

normally be easier to land when hooked at an offshore paddy as compared to a coastal kelp bed. Around the floating paddy that may be no more than the size of a doormat, there isn't any other structure to worry about. But where there are kelp beds there are often rocks, and either one can prematurely give the fish its freedom. Therefore, even though the size of the fish may be the same in both locations, you'll need two different size outfits to accommodate the different set of conditions.

Just as golfers cannot play a round with the same club, there is no one fly rod that can do it all. You may as well resign yourself to the fact that you are going to need more than one rod. As you can see in the examples above, even if you plan to fish only one species, different conditions dictate different flies and fly lines and this in turn will necessitate the use of different size rods. As in most consumer decisions, it's not always easy to distinguish needs from wants. New products are constantly on the market and even though you may not need a new rod, it's nice to fish with the latest model. But a word of caution is in order here. You might find that the new rod doesn't cast or fish as well as a previous model which may no longer be available. That happens with a lot of goods. So maybe it's a good idea to follow the advice of one of my friends who subscribes to the philosophy that if you buy something you really like, if you can afford to, buy two. I have done that with fly rods. One of my all-time favorite heavy-duty rods is the Great Equalizer. It was available through Scientific Anglers and Lefty Kreh had a lot to do with its design. You would have a difficult time finding one now. I have two, including an original of Lefty's and I'll never part with them. I seldom fish with them now, partly because of their value as collector items and the fact that there are rods available today that are as good or better. But for many years, there wasn't anything out there that could match these sticks and I treasured them like icons.

In terms of line size, if I were restricted to one rod only for inshore saltwater fly-fishing, almost irrespective of locale or species, it would be a 9-weight. I think this is the most versatile rod, one that will enable you to effectively target practically every available species you're likely to encounter with the exception of large tarpon and offshore brutes like billfish and tuna. If you have the option of acquiring two rods (and I'll bet that most newcomers to the sport will eventually arrive at this point) then I would choose a combination like an 8- and 10-weight or a 9- and an 11-weight. Again, with the exception of big, blue-water fish, for most of the conditions in coastal waters you don't have much need for anything heavier than an 11-weight rod.

Fly Reels

At the risk of raising some folk's eyebrows, I'll go on record as arguing that for the lion's share of most coastal fly-fishing, I do not assign the fly reel the same degree of importance as I do the rod. As previously stated, the rod is the principal fish-fighting and delivery system. We don't need the reel to cast or manipulate the fly. And while the reel must certainly function as more than a mere storage receptacle for the line, for most situations, the reel's importance as a fish-fighting mechanism is not as critical as it is for rods. Its most important attribute is a smooth, utterly consistent drag mechanism. For years I got by with the single-action System reels that were marketed by Scientific Anglers. These were manufactured by the venerable Hardy Brothers of England and they served me well on everything from

striped bass to sharks. By today's standards, they're almost primitive but I still like fishing them on occasion. It's sort of like having an antique car. Once in a while you like to take it out for a weekend spin but you wouldn't want to use it as your primary means of transportation. Besides, today you have so many great reels from which to choose.

Corbett Davis, Jr. with a nice Louisiana red.

In this respect, I'm also very fortunate to have teamed up with one of the most respected manufacturers in the industry. Soon after graduate school when my financial situation began to improve, I started buying the Billy Pate reels designed and manufactured by the master machinist, Ted Juracsik. Way back in the mid-sixties and early seventies, the premier reel was the SeaMaster, but the supply was extremely limited and you could have a reel on order for years. It was on a fishing trip with Lefty down at Casa Mar where I first became acquainted with Ted's reels. Lefty loaned me his Tarpon model for a day's fishing with the silver kings and I didn't want to give it back. When I returned home I bought one of the first models. It was heavy and you could literally drive nails with it—I actually did this fishing out of skiffs in Baja that had more loose screws than an asylum. The reel has never failed me. The drag has never been replaced and to this day it is still fished hard. Its new home is with Captain Joe Blados in eastern Long Island. He was telling me how he needed a reliable, bullet-proof reel for his charter business and I gave him the reel. Realizing that it was my first, Joe was reluctant to take it but I assured him that Ted builds his reels to be fished, not to be sitting around as collector's items. And something you don't find with most reel makers, if for whatever reason you wanted to modify the reel, even an old one like this is retro-fittable to current production models.

After that first Tarpon model, I bought the Bonefish, the Marlin and the Bluefin. The latter two models I use strictly for big-game fishing, but the one that had seen the most use was the Bonefish. Sadly I lost it on a shark fishing trip when I had a boat in King Harbor in Redondo Beach. From the standpoint of line capacity, the Bonefish model is not designed for shark fishing, but everything else in the construction of the reel is well up to the task. I was catching plenty of blue sharks in those days, spiced with an occasional mako. My standard outfit was a heavy-duty 12-weight, but this day I wanted to fool around with lighter gear so I brought along a 9-weight Lamiglass rod and matched it to the Pate Bonefish reel. A friend I brought along just released about a six-foot blue that took his fly drifting in the chum slick. I was going to take my turn with the 9-weight outfit when he called me up to the bow to help him tie a new leader. I made the foolish mistake of leaning the rod on the gunwale and did not realize that the fly was dangling in the water next to the wire basket that held the chum. I always make it a practice never to fish with a tight drag, but the slight resistance I had it set at was sufficient to enable the shark to jerk the outfit overboard when it took the fly.

A few years ago Ted started to build a new series of reels under his own name (Tibor) and naturally I had to have one. He sent me an early model Everglades to test and I couldn't find anything negative to report. This model and the slightly larger Riptide are the reels I most often fish. I didn't have one at the time, but for a trip to Midway Island a few years ago I recommended that a friend of mine buy the Gulf stream. With a line capacity of 300 yards of 30-pound micron backing and a full weight-forward floating 12-weight line, the Gulf stream is the largest model in the Tibor lineup. Though most of the giant amber jack and trevalley managed to cut him off on the coral, the reel functioned flawlessly, fish after fish. I have another friend whose passion is yellowfin tuna and this is his reel of choice.

The Tibors and Pates like other fine reels such as the Able, Charlton, and Islander are not inexpensive and for most inshore applications at least, you can get by with less pricey models. If however, you are looking for something that will last a lifetime and then some, these reels are worth your consideration.

Regardless of how much you are prepared to spend, there are a number of factors you should look for in a saltwater fly reel. First of all, in contrast to conventional and spinning reels, most fly reels are single action. That means the retrieve ratio is 1:1 (one full turn of the handle yields one complete revolution of the spool). There are multiplier reels available and they do permit

Bill Barnes releases a tarpon for one of his guests at Casa Mar.

more rapid line retrieval. But the downside is more complicated gearing and added weight. As is true with most mechanical devices, the simplest design is often the best and that is certainly the case with fly reels. Instead of buying a multiplier, one way to facilitate more rapid line retrieval is to select a reel with a large arbor. Because a larger-diameter spool takes in more line with every revolution, I make it a practice to use a larger-size reel than the one normally recommended for a particular rod-and-reel combination. Some manufacturers designate their reels according to fly-line sizes, like a 7/8 model or a 9/10. Unfortunately, the fly tackle industry has not standardized these designations, but as a rule you can opt for the next larger size reel and still have a balanced outfit. Thus, if I am using an 8-weight rod, I mate it with a 9/10 size reel. As another example, Ted Juracsik designates the Everglades model as ideally suited for rod weights 7 to 9. The next larger model is the Riptide rated for 9- to 11-weight rods. What I often do is mount the Riptide on an 8-weight rod. It balances fine. I have more line capacity than I'll ever need, but more importantly, when the need arises, I can crank in line very rapidly. I've been with Bob Popovics when he's used the Gulf stream on a 9- and 10-weight rod fishing striped bass. He likes the ability to retrieve line quickly with a minimum of turns on the handle.

Another way to determine reel size is according to its designated line capacity. A reel that will hold approximately 200 yards of 30-pound-test Dacron backing will handle basically all your inshore needs. For the offshore grounds, where there's the chance for bigger fish, a larger capacity reel that will hold more than 250 yards of line is a better choice.

A feature that is particularly useful for inshore applications, particularly when fishing the surf, is the ability to quickly change spools. When fishing from a boat, it's usually not a problem to have a number of fully rigged outfits on hand, but this isn't practical for the shore-bound angler. Carrying an extra spool is generally not a major inconvenience, but it can be a real hassle if the spool cannot be easily removed and replaced. Even if you do not have to change spools, a quick take-apart feature makes it easy to clean the reel. Anytime you hit the beach you can bet that sand will eventually work its way into the reel and being able to simply pop the spool off and wipe away any foreign particles saves a lot of frustration. Ted's latest offering, the Tibor Light, designed for 3- to 6-weight rods, has a spool that is easily removable via a large retaining knob. That feature coupled with its great drag and corrosion-proof parts makes it a favorite of mine for light-tackle beach fishing.

A number of reels that feature easy spool removal also have exposed spool rims. All Ted's reels from the tiny Trout model to the Bluefin incorporate this feature. This enables you to augment the reel's drag mechanism by palming the rim to instantly increase or decrease resistance to the spool. In fact, as I've preached in countless fly-fishing schools over the years, your hand and fingers make for the best drag system. This is simply because they can regulate the resistance against the spool faster and with more control than is possible with any mechanical system. The purpose of the reel's drag mechanism is not to stop a fish from running. Instead, its function is to provide controlled resistance. That is why you never want to fish with the reel's drag completely locked tight. You will not be able to react fast enough to back off on it when a fish suddenly decides to bolt away to gain its freedom. Most accomplished anglers will tell you that they fish with the lightest drag pressure possible, often only enough to prevent the line from over-running the spool (commonly referred to as a backlash). In quantitative terms this translates into less than a pound of drag pressure. Any additional pressure is applied by hand.

Fly reels are available in both right- and left-hand retrieve and here there should be no question as to which one you should choose. Nevertheless, it is a question I am frequently asked and my response is very straightforward. If we were playing baseball, unless you were a switch hitter, you would never ask which way to bat. A right-hander would bat right-handed and a lefty would bat left-handed. And that is exactly how it should be with fly reels. The trouble is, many novice fly-fishers have been erroneously led to believe that if they are right-handed casters, they should wind with their left eliminating the need to switch the rod to the left hand when they want to begin winding line in. Forgive me, but this is nonsense. If you cannot perform this simple maneuver, you probably shouldn't be fly-fishing in the first place. The plain fact of the matter is that most people who are right-handed cannot reel as effectively with their left hand and vice versa. There are occasions when a fish suddenly reverses direction and runs straight at you. Here is where you have to wind furiously to recover the slack line as quickly as possible. If you cannot do this for sustained periods with your left hand, do not use a left-hand wind reel. With most of today's reels it's easy to convert to right- or left-hand drive.

One final option to note is the choice between direct-drive and anti-reverse fly reels. In the former, the handle spins backward as line is peeled from the spool. Though there aren't many available today, years ago direct-drive conventional reels were commonplace. It doesn't take much imagination to determine how they earned the nickname, "knuckle buster." Practically all contemporary conventional and spinning reels are anti-reverse or at least have anti-reverse mechanisms. However, perhaps partly due to tradition, most fly reels are direct drive, but there are anti-reverse models available. If you have never used a direct-drive reel, you will find that they take a little getting used to. You have to train yourself to keep your fingers away from the spinning handle. Why put up with this if you have the option of buying an anti-reverse model? Well, the main advantage to a direct-drive reel is that line retrieval is absolutely positive. Every time you turn the reel handle, you pick up line. That isn't necessarily the case with anti-reverse models. With a light drag setting you can turn the handle, but there may be slippage and the spool will not turn. For that reason my personal preference is for direct drive. It only takes a little experience to develop the habit of keeping your fingers out of harm's way.

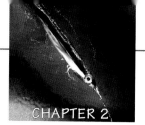
Laying It On The Line: Backing, Fly Line And Leader Basics

The one component in the tackle system that most clearly differentiates fly-fishing from other forms of angling is the fly line. With conventional and spinning gear, it is the concentrated weight of the bait or lure that carries the line during the cast. In fly-fishing however, it is a weighted fly line that carries the fly. Instead of being concentrated at one point, the weight is distributed along a long length of line. Fly lines are sized according to their weight in grains and are assigned numerical designations on that basis. For example, an 8-weight line has a grain weight of 210, a 10-weight weighs 280 grains. Fly rods and fly-line weights are standardized which makes it easy to put together a balanced outfit. Nine-weight rods for example, are designed to cast 9-weight fly lines. However, a good-quality fly rod can handle higher line weights than the one specified by the manufacturer and many anglers find casting a bit easier if they overload their rod by one or two line weights. So, if your rod is a 9-weight, it should easily cast a 10-weight line.

Two other properties of fly lines you must consider are their taper and their ability to float or sink. The taper determines the casting characteristics of the fly line. There are a variety of choices, but for most of my saltwater fly-fishing, I find that I still revert to basically two types, a weight-forward and a shooting taper. A weight-forward line (WF) is a full line, generally 90 feet in length. The weighted portion of the line is confined to the first 30 feet, referred to as the head section. It consists of a fairly short front taper, a belly section (this is the

Seeing red.

large-diameter section of line where most of the weight is concentrated), and a short rear taper. Compared to a double line (DT) which many dry-fly, trout enthusiasts prefer for delicate presentations, a weight-forward line will enable you to make longer casts. An accomplished caster can throw the full 90 feet of fly line. However, as the sport began to develop, anglers started to encounter situations where they had to make comparatively long casts with a minimum of effort. This is where the shooting head comes into play.

Shooting heads were developed in the Pacific Northwest by salmon and steelhead fishermen who had to present their flies across broad stretches of river. The more water they could cover, the better their chances of intercepting fish. Standard weight-forward lines could not deliver the distance they needed, hence the development of the shooting head. A shooting head is designed to maximize distance with a minimum of false casting. This is accomplished by combining what are essentially two different lines. The shooting head, or shooting taper as it is sometimes referred to, is similar to the larger-diameter portion (the belly) of a weight-forward line. Typically then, most shooting heads are 30 feet in length. However, unlike a full, continuous line, this head is joined to a completely separate, small-diameter running line and it is this combination that affords longer casts than normally possible with a conventional full-length, weight-forward fly line.

Today however, there are full-length lines that function much like a shooting head. In conjunction with my good friend Trey Combs, Jim Vincent of Rio Fly Lines, has recently introduced a new full-length line called the DeepSea Line. It is available in grain weights of 200, 300, 400, 500 and 600. The 200-grain weight line is fine for light-tackle inshore applications, however the ones I use most for coastal fishing with 9-, 10- and 11-weight rods, are the 300- and 400-grain lines. Even for most offshore situations, you generally will not need anything heavier than the 500-grain line. Each of these lines has an overall length of 100 feet. The super-fast sinking, density-compensated head is 26 1/2 feet, immediately followed by a heavy intermediate body/back taper which makes it very easy to cast. The running line section has a monofilament braided core with a smooth, hard coating which is very resistant to tangles. On that score alone, I highly recommend it.

A similar line of this type that I can also recommend is the appropriately named Depth Finder from AirFlo. My good friend, Iain Sorrel who is the distributor for the U.S., first showed me this line at one of Bob Marriott's Fly-fishing Fairs and I came away quite impressed. This is also a 100-foot line that is available in 200- to 600-grain weights. But what distinguishes this line from the others is a new higher density coating that gives the 30-foot head section a 15 to 20% faster sink rate for any given grain weight. It has a floating running section and thus far I have found it to be relatively tangle free even under a variety of different water temperatures. I don't know how it would handle in some of the very cold temperatures you can encounter in steelhead fishing, but as far as I'm concerned, the point is mute because I'm no longer fond of subjecting myself to that kind of abuse. When water temperature starts to fall below the high 50s, I start thinking of other pastimes.

Another full-length line I am impressed with is Scientific Anglers' new fast-sinking, Striper IV. Do not let its name fool you. With a sink rate of 3.75 to 6.5 inches per second, this 120-foot line is ideally suited for situations well beyond the realm of striper fishing. Available in weights 7 to 13, this series will handle just about every set of conditions you're likely to encounter from back bays to blue water. The Striper IV also features a braided mono running line that very seldom tangles, a quality that will spare you considerable frustration when you're out on the water.

In comparison to a shooting head, the only drawback to these lines is the fact that their one continuous length makes changing lines a bit of problem. To completely unravel 100-plus feet of fly line takes some time and is best done in a relatively obstacle-free environment. A full-length line is also more cumbersome to coil and store neatly in a small compartment like a shirt or vest pocket. It might be easier to switch to a different outfit or use a spare spool. If you are on a boat where spare outfits are readily on hand, the DeepSea and Striper IV are my lines of choice when I want to get the fly down in a hurry. However, if you are fishing from the beach or breakwater where it is impractical to carry additional outfits or spare spool, the quick change shooting-head system may be a more practical choice. Since all you are working with is a 30-foot section of line, changing from one head to another is a relatively simple process. Rio has addressed this problem with the introduction of their new Leviathan VersiTip system. This line is simply the interchangeable head version of the DeepSea fly line. The running-line section has a heavy taper that can be used with different Leviathan tips. These tip sections are available in weights from 200 to 700 grains, but the ones I find most useful are the 300-, 400-, and 500-grain heads.

To effect these quick changes you'll need a loop-to-loop connection in the shooting-head system. Most of the shooting head systems from the major fly-line manufacturers have factory-installed loops at the rear end of the head section. I also prefer a loop in the front end so I can make leader changes without having to cut the line. In addition, if you want to change the length of the heads or substitute different running lines, you'll have to make your own loops.

One of the best methods of making loops in a coated fly line or shooting head involves the use of nail knots tied with 8- to 12-pound-test mono. Simply fold the fly line over itself to form the desired loop (a half-inch loop is about right). Then bind the two sections together by tying a 7- or 8-turn nail knot. Tie a second knot approximately 1/16 to 1/8 inch behind the first. The mono cuts slightly into the fly-line's coating making for a very strong loop. I have had the fly line break, but the loop has never pulled free. The only glue I use in the process is a flexible adhesive like Pliobond or Loon's Knot Sense to coat the knots. The adhesive is not for strength, it protects the mono from abrasion and makes for a smooth connection.

Some of the heavy grain heads can be fairly large in diameter and if you simply folded the line back on itself, the result would be a relatively bulky connection that might have difficulty passing smoothly through the rod guides. In situations like these, strip away about 2 inches of the line's coating, exposing the inner core. This can be accomplished in several ways. If you have it on hand, you can soak the end of the fly line in acetone for about 20 seconds. The shell can then be peeled off with your fingernail. Alternatively, tie a 1 1/2-foot section of 8-pound mono around the fly line with a double overhand knot. Cinch the knot down tightly, grasp both ends of the mono and jerk it toward the end of the line. This should strip off the coating. You can do the same thing by tying a girth hitch in a length of 20-pound Dacron. With the core exposed, fold the line over itself to form the loop and secure it with nail knots.

With lead-core heads, there are two methods I use for making end loops. One simple technique involves working out about 5 inches of lead filament from the braid. Alternately push down on the braid while gently pulling up on the exposed lead. Break off the lead, fold the braid back over itself and tie a double overhand (surgeon's) knot in the braid. The nail knot technique can also be used. Remove a section of lead, fold the braid back over itself and bind it together with nail knots. With some lead-core lines there is no coating for the mono to imbed itself in so to compensate for this, I tie 3 to 4 separate nail knots. You will not experience any failures this way. The type of loop I fasten in the running line is a function of the type of line being used. Bear in mind that there is no such thing as a perfect

A Bahamas bone.

running line. All of them have their pluses as well as their drawbacks.

A very smooth line and one that will afford maximum distance is a mono running line. They vary in terms of finish and flexibility and thus far, the one I like best is Rio's Slick Shooter. For the best results, you'll want to thoroughly stretch this line prior to use. Rigging a mono shooting line is a very simple process. To form a loop all you have to do is fold the line over itself and tie a 3-turn surgeon's knot.

Rio's new MonoCore shooting line rivals the monofilament lines in terms of smoothness, but I have not had a chance to use these lines in actual fishing conditions. The exciting thing about this industry is that you have plenty of options, and you can be sure that every year, some new product will hit the market.

The coated running lines are fairly small in diameter so I make loops using the same nail knot method described for the shooting head. Hollow-core braided lines also make good running lines. Because they are virtually memory-free, they work especially well when you are using a stripping basket. However, they can be very abrasive when repeatedly stripped across your finger and for that reason I recommend a two-handed retrieve when using these lines.

You can fashion some very smooth loops in these lines by means of an eye splice. A splicing tool is easily made from a 12-inch piece of 27-pound-test single-strand wire. Fold the wire in half and pinch it at the juncture of the bend. This will make it easy to insert into the braid. Make the insertion approximately 6 inches from the tag end of the braid. Work the wire into the braid about 1 1/2 inches going toward the tag end. Push the wire out through the braid, catch the tag end inside the wire loop and pull it down through the same 1 1/2-inch section. Pull the wire and tag end out through the braid. By carefully pulling on the tag end, you can form the desired-size loop in the braid (generally between 1/2 to 3/4 inches). As an extra measure of security, I work the wire into the braid a second time. Approximately an inch below the point where the tag end was pulled out from the center of the braid, insert the wire and push it up through the braid. Push it out through the braid, catch the tag end in the wire loop and pull it down through the braid. To make absolutely certain the loop will never pull free, bind the base of the loop with a mono nail knot.

About the only possible disadvantage to a shooting head is in some floating-line applications. With a conventional weight-forward floating line, it's possible to lift a long length of line off the water and make another cast. This isn't possible with a floating shooting head. Instead, most of the running line will have to be stripped in before you can lift the head from the water. The small-diameter running line cannot support the heavy head. So generally speaking, if you have more than about 5 feet or so of this line outside the rod tip, the line begins to sag and the head will be difficult to cast. For this reason, if a floating line is needed, I generally use a full-length weight forward.

However, it's a different story where sinking lines are involved. With a line that slips below the surface, regardless of whether it's a head or full-length line, most of the line including the heavy belly section will have to be stripped in before you can set up for the next cast. You cannot simply lift a long section of line off the water like you do with a floater. Therefore, when sinking lines are called for, a full-length, weight-forward line offers no casting advantage over a shooting head. Many anglers have difficulty with sinking lines because they fail to realize that the line has to be brought back to the surface before they can cast. I'll go over that in Chapter 5 where I take up the subject of casting.

With the exception of fishing shallow-water flats and working surface poppers, the shooting head is generally my primary fly line choice for salt water. As mentioned above, about the only time I go to a full-length, weight-forward line is when I want to fish a floating line. When I lived in Southern California, my opportunity to fish these lines was very limited because there was so little surface action. That's all changed now that I'm back in the Northeast where there are stripers and blues eager to take top-water offerings. However, even here I still find that most of the action is subsurface and you will find this to be the case practically anywhere you fish. Therefore, if you want to maximize your chances of consistently getting into fish, you will have to use sinking lines.

What many anglers fail to realize is that even when you see fish breaking on top, most of the feeding activity is taking place at least a few feet below. Some will bring up the fact that a floating line with a weighted fly like a Clouser or a Popovics Jiggy will slip several feet below the surface. True, but the point is that it often takes too long. When you fish salt water you have to contend with current and current can significantly impede a fly's sink rate. Even lines designated as fast sinking do not plunge into the depths as rapidly as a lead sinker or metal jig. So even when fish are surface feeding and all you have is a fast-sinking line, simply start stripping in the fly as soon as it hits the water. It won't sink very far and you'll still be in the feeding zone. Most of the time when you have to get the fly down, you want it to sink as quickly as possible. That is why I recommend fast-sinking lines for most sub-surface fishing. If for some reason you want to slow the fly's descent, use a buoyant pattern like the Blados Crease Fly or Popovics' Cotton Candy (these and other productive patterns will be taken up in Chapter 4).

There are two additional advantages to sinking lines. Their smaller diameter takes up less space on the spool so you can fill the reel with more backing. Also, their thinner profile makes them easier to cast into the wind than floating lines. To further enhance their casting effectiveness, I follow the overload principle mentioned earlier. Just like full-length lines, shooting heads have numerical designations and I generally step up to the next size line weight.

Since the final forward cast should be executed with the shooting head totally outside the rod tip, I tend to favor those lines that are not more than 30 feet in length. Any longer than that and they become difficult to handle. Bear in mind, that a head is designed to maximize casting efficiency. This means that false casts are kept to a minimum. If the head is too long it may take an extra false cast or two to work it out through the rod tip. This wastes time. In addition, if you are fishing a steep-sloping beach (and these are often the most productive stretches), a head that is too long can result in problems on the back cast if it causes you to strike the beach or other obstacles behind you. This can dull the hook point, fray the leader or even break the fly off. Shorter heads minimize these problems.

The shooting heads marketed by line companies like Cortland, Rio and Scientific Anglers are 30 feet in length. To make them even more user-friendly, I used to shorten them a bit by cutting two to three feet of line from the rear end of the line. For example, if I wanted to fish a 9-weight rod, I would take an 11-weight shooting head and cut it to 28 feet. However, with Rio's Leviathan VersiTip system, I no longer find this necessary. The tip sections are 26 feet which I find ideal for most situations where I want to use a shooting head. For maximum distance I substitute the smaller-diameter Slick Shooter running line for the heavier taper line that is supplied with the system. Either way, you'll find these shorter heads are very easy to cast.

Lead-core lines are the least expensive of all lines. They have some of the fastest sink rates. These are level lines with no tapers so you don't have to be careful about which end to cut. Unfortunately, lead-core lines are not standardized and they come packaged on spools in continuous lengths that may be as long as one hundred yards. Depending on the yardage, you can make up a lot of shooting heads, but each will have to be cut to accommodate different size rods. As a guideline, I've found that with most lead-core brands, 23 feet balances nicely with 8- and 9-weight rods. Eleven- and 12-weight rods should easily cast lines in the 24- to 27-foot range. Lead-core is available in different breaking strengths and for most of our fishing you can select lines in the 27- to 40-pound-test category.

Leaders

The leader serves as the connection between the fly and the fly line. Never cast a fly line without a leader, even if

CAPTAIN JOE BLADOS

you are just practicing. The leader transmits the energy from the fly line during the cast. A leader with no fly attached will fray. That's what will happen to the tag end of the fly line if you cast with no leader.

Leaders are constructed with monofilament line and aside from the fact that they tend to be less visible in the water than most fly lines, their main function is twofold. The leader serves to lessen the impact of the fly line on the water and it enables the fly to turn over properly at the conclusion of the forward cast. In many situations when you're fishing salt water you don't have to be too concerned about delicacy of presentation. But this is not the case anytime you fish clear, shallow water. Here the manner in which the line strikes the surface can be critical. Bonefish flats are the classic example, but for years in Southern California if I didn't want to travel far, the closest I could come to conditions like this was fishing corbina on a tidal bar right after sunrise. The wind is usually down and even though you are in the surf zone, the water is often relatively calm and clear. It's fairly shallow, seldom more than knee deep. This is where I would use a clear, intermediate-sinking fly line. It is less visible in the water than other fly lines. But corbina can still spook easily if there is any unnatural surface disturbance. Therefore, you don't want the line to come crashing down on the water. To help avoid this, I would tie on a long, tapered leader (about 9 feet) much like the one I use for bonefishing in the tropics.

Something you want to take note of when tying your own leaders is the fact that leader material from different manufacturers is not uniform. For a given pound test they may vary in diameter and stiffness. This kind of mismatch could result in a hinge effect when you cast and the leader will not turn over properly. To prevent this, make sure to tie all your leader sections with the same material. Start with a five-foot section of 50-pound test. This is referred to as the butt section. I like to connect this to the fly line via a loop-to-loop connection. That way I can change the leader simply by unlocking loops without having to cut either the fly line or the leader. This butt section is followed by foot-long segments of 40-, 30- and 25-pound test. To facilitate quick changes in the final class tippet section, at the tag end of the 25-pound-test segment, you can tie a surgeon's loop. This loop is interconnected with the loop in the last section of leader, an 18- to 24-inch length of class tippet. However, if you don't like having a loop at this juncture (and I personally do not), just tie the class tippet directly to the 25-pound-test segment. The fly is tied directly to the tag end of the class tippet. In the following chapter I'll take up the subject of knots and show you how to tie all these connections.

For most other conditions where you'll be using sinking lines, a shorter, non-tapered leader is all you need. Many anglers make the mistake of using long leaders with their sinking lines. What they don't realize is that a long leader defeats the purpose of a sinking line. The long leader will develop a bow with the fly streaming above the sinking line. Generally, when fishing sinking lines, my leaders are only about three feet. Many times I do not even use a butt section, just the class tippet. I tie a Bimini twist in one end of the class tippet, twist the loop that has been formed, fold the loop over itself and tie a surgeon's loop. This yields a two-stand loop that is interlocked directly to the end loop in the fly line. If the leader starts getting too short because you're cutting it periodically to change flies, simply replace it with another. To save time on the water, I have at least a half dozen Bimini leaders tied and ready to go.

Tackle Maintenance

From boats to buoys, there are virtually no man made objects that can stand up to the effects of salt water without at least a minimum of care. Today's saltwater rods, reels and lines do amazingly well in this environment, but to maintain everything at its peak, periodically they will require some cleaning and lubrication. The good news is that compared to more complex systems like boats and motors, none of this will take more than a few minutes of your time.

Fly lines and backing do not corrode but they are subject to an accumulation of salt crystals. They will be much more pleasant to fish with if you clean everything off after each trip. All you have to do is strip off the line that has been immersed in the salt and hose it off with fresh water. You can do this on your lawn, at the dock or even in the shower.

I do the same with my rods. Just be sure to dry the rod thoroughly if you plan on storing it in a cloth bag otherwise mildew will likely develop. Before I ever fish the rod, I apply small dabs of grease to the reel seat grooves. This will prevent the lock washers from freezing up on you. Even though rods from name-brand manufacturers are incredibly durable, they are not indestructible. If they are banged around a lot they can develop small cracks and fissures and this could

eventually result in breakage. To help prevent this, use a sturdy rod case to transport your rods. Most of the boats designed for fly-fishing have built-in compartments that totally envelop the rod.

The ferruling system on today's rods are far superior to those of yesteryear, but you still want to be careful in putting rod sections together. The proper way is to first align a top, or "female", section at a ninety-degree angle from the bottom ("male") section. Then simultaneously rotate and press the top section into the bottom section. Never jam two sections together. A half turn is about all it takes to have the guides from the different sections in proper alignment. Periodically you should lubricate the male ferrule with candle wax or paraffin.

It's OK to wash off the line and rod with a high-pressure hose, but you don't want to do this with reels. The water pressure will drive foreign particles into places they normally wouldn't get to. Instead, use a cloth or sponge soaked in warm water and wipe the reel down with it. Warm water helps break down the salt particles. A little mild detergent soap will really get things clean. Occasionally apply a light lubricating oil to the reel handle and a dollop of grease to the spool's shaft. And after each outing, make sure to loosen the drag-adjustment knob. If left tight, the drag washers can be deformed.

CAPTAIN JOE BLADOS

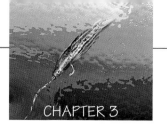

CHAPTER 3

Knots You Should Know

Not long ago, a student in one of my fly-fishing classes who was having a little difficulty trying to master a particular knot, suddenly blurted out, "I'm knot impaired." We all had a good laugh. Hopefully this chapter will help you avoid this condition.

If your financial status is a little shaky, it may be difficult to justify spending large sums just for the privilege of fishing with expensive custom-crafted rods and reels. As I pointed out in the chapter on tackle, there is a wide selection of excellent-quality gear tailored to moderate budgets and in most situations the performance is equal to that of their pricier counterparts. However, when it comes to making connections in the backing, fly line and leader systems, using the very best knots is something that everyone can afford. In fact, it is something you cannot afford to neglect because improper or poorly tied knots can have disastrous consequences. The line system is the vital connection between you and the fish. In the battle phase of the contest, rod breakage or reel failure is not something you usually have to worry about. Furthermore, even in the worst case scenario with a rod or reel mishap, it may still be possible to hand line the fish into submission. But if the line fails, the game is immediately terminated.

More so than other components in the tackle system, lines are subject to constant wear, particularly the leader section. Despite sophisticated manufacturing techniques, there are times when even a brand-new unknotted line simply breaks when it should not have. Fortunately, this is a rare occurrence, but I have had it happen. Fish of course, will do their utmost to gain their freedom. They read the encounter as a life-or-death contest and if there is a way to rid themselves of this terrifying string they are tethered to, they will certainly give it a try. Their naturally equipped body parts in the form of teeth, gill plates, fins and scales can quickly sever a leader. Then

The author with a Casa Mar jungle giant.

depending on locale, there's an endless array of potential hazards ranging from rocks to boat keels that can wear down a line like a dog chewing on a beef bone. Even with excellent fish-fighting technique, line cuts and abrasion will inevitably take their toll, but knot failure shouldn't be part of the equation.

I don't know if it ranks as intelligence as we define it, or just the instinct to survive, but I can recount numerous instances where fish used structure such as rocks, coral and pilings to deliberately try and sever the connection. California yellowtail are particularly adept at this. If statistics were kept on such matters, I know of a rock outcropping off San Martin Island in northern Baja that would be in contention for fraying the most lines in yellowtail fishing. If you anchor off the southern tip of the rock, every yellow you hook heads straight for the partially exposed rock and then turns sharply to the left to skirt its jagged edge. I've fished this spot for over 30 years, mostly with stout conventional tackle, and can testify that even large-diameter 60-pound-test monofilament line will break like sewing thread being drawn across a razor blade if it makes contact with the rock. I've hooked several on fly here, but never succeeded in bringing any to the boat. Most of the time I could see where the leader made contact with the rock. It felt like it was worked over with a sander. A couple of times when the yellows made a slightly wider turn, the leader stayed intact but the fly line was cut in half. That's an expensive loss and even though they're not in the business of selling lines, I'm convinced that yellowtail know exactly what they have to do to terminate unwanted connections. There is no place for them to take refuge around the rock. So the only reason I can see for them heading there is that Mother Nature somehow programmed them to take advantage of this imposing piece of structure in the event they ever became encumbered by a strand of human technology called fishing line.

Bill Barnes also has some interesting stories to tell in this regard, far removed from fishing yellowtail in Baja. Bill has the distinction of landing several double-digit bonefish at a flat in the Bahamas, the exact location of which he is understandably reluctant to divulge. The bones he's managed to boat and release all showed signs of recently bruised lips embedded with sand and marl. It was apparent that in an effort to get rid of the fly, these big and obviously savvy bonefish, rubbed their snouts in

the bottom. Using non-stainless hooks, the fly would eventually dislodge, but their immediate freedom was won by effectively fraying the line to the point where it eventually broke. With the few he's been able to land, Bill considers himself lucky because in every case several inches of the 12-pound mono class tippet was severely abraded.

To ensure a strong, reliable connection between the different sections in your line system requires little more than average manual dexterity and the willingness to spend some time to master the tying sequences. A friend of mine had a good deal of the former but lacked the

CAPTAIN JOE BLADOS

discipline to learn a few important knots and it cost him dearly on a trip we made to Casa Mar lodge in Costa Rica. This fellow was a former student of mine at the university and given his pattern of procrastination and frantic last-ditch efforts to complete assignments, I wasn't surprised at his reluctance to take the time to learn how to tie tarpon leaders. We were going through them like toothpicks at a popcorn festival. I had tied dozens prior to the trip and he found it a lot more convenient to dip into my tackle bag and simply take whatever he needed. On the fourth day of our week-long trip, the tarpon turned on at the river mouth but the surf was very high which meant that we had to fight these 80-pound-plus silver kings from an anchored boat just inside the entrance to the river. Trying to stop tarpon this size from running through the raging currents presented a supreme challenge. I would guess that we managed to keep the fly planted in about 70 percent of the fish we hooked, but of that number, at least half eventually won their freedom by making it out past the river mouth. Out in the open sea, the tarpon kept running and if you couldn't turn them back toward the mouth, they would strip all the line from the spool. To prevent this, I used class tippets with 16-pound breaking strengths. With 30-pound-test Dacron backing, 40-pound running line and a 40-pound-test lead-core shooting head, the 16-pound tippet represented the weak link in my line system. If anything broke, I wanted it to be the easily replaceable leader. Of course this is all premised on the condition that there are proper connections between the different line segments ensuring their maximum rated breaking strengths. I'll show you how to do this in this chapter. My friend didn't have to bother because I pre-rigged all his lines and in his mind there seemed to be an endless supply of leaders. If we couldn't turn the tarpon back toward the mouth, we simply applied enough pressure to pop the tippet. When it broke, all we had to do was reel in all the line the fish ran out, loop on a new leader, tie on another fly and get back in the action.

I didn't count how many tarpon we parted company with, but at the end of the day there were only a few remaining leaders and that evening after dinner I spent several hours tying up new ones for the next day's fishing. I encouraged my friend to sit with me and learn how to tie the necessary connections but the pina coladas and the attentions of a young lady who recently arrived with her father proved a far more attractive proposition. I reminded him that we planned to forego lunch the next day so we could fish off the beach at the river mouth and that if the tarpon were still in a feeding mood, we would need plenty of leaders. His response was, "You tie them so fast, you'll have a bunch ready in no time. If you try to show me now, it will waste too much time." This was typical of the reasoning mode he applied to many of his classroom assignments. In those cases he earned only mediocre grades. But on the beach the next day, he was about to learn a more dramatic lesson.

The tarpon were moving through the river mouth like customers going through a checkout stand at a tag sale. Fishing from the skiff that morning was one of the best days I ever experienced on the water. There were three other boats anchored to our right and every few minutes there was at least one fish in the air. The sound of their large silver sides smacking the water reminded me of the naval ships in San Diego harbor dropping their anchors. As is often the case in tarpon fishing, I would estimate that approximately 50 percent of the fish were prematurely released primarily as a result of their ability to dislodge the hook. But with non-stop action, the disappointment was short lived and by noon everyone was ready to take a lunch break back at the lodge. Everyone except my friend and I. The skiff fishing was phenomenal but I wanted to experience the thrill of hooking and battling tarpon from a standing position along the beach at the entrance to the river mouth. Not many anglers have had this privilege and I didn't want to lose this rare opportunity.

Around 11:30 when the other boats pulled anchor and headed back for the lodge, our guide slid the flat-bottomed john boat up on the wet sand and my friend and I stepped off with our tackle and a couple of box lunches. We should not have bothered to take the food because we never had an opportunity to eat any of it. The dorsal and tail fins of surfacing tarpon were piercing the surface along the entire edge of the beach not more than 20 yards from where we were standing. To give ourselves enough room, we put about 100 feet between us and began casting and fishing our flies upstream to allow them to sink a few feet before being swept into the mouth by the strong current flowing seaward. This is a method I've used often fishing salmon, but even 40-pound kings in fast-flowing rivers never seemed to stop the fly with the same authority as these shore-cruising tarpon. In all my years of fishing afoot, I never experienced anything like this. As any shore-bound angler will tell you, hooking and battling fish when you're standing on terra firma is an almost magical experience. Maybe it has something to do with the intimate mix of two very different realms, a curious blend of land and water augmented with the connection between the inhabitants of both worlds in the form of angler and fish.

Aside from the special sensation of hooking and fighting these awesome fish from the beach, in this case being shore bound proved to be an advantage because it provided a degree of mobility that wasn't possible from a stationary boat. I couldn't follow the fish through the surf line, but I could jog along the edge of the river mouth, a tactic that saved about 60 yards of line that would have been stripped off by the tarpon if it were hooked from a boat anchored well behind the opening. Generally, the less line you allow a fish to make off with in its run for freedom, the better your chances of being able to eventually subdue it. I'm convinced that two of the big tarpon I was finally able to slide up on the wet sand were landed because I could keep pace with them on foot before they swam too far out through the turbulent mouth.

Nonetheless, despite this important advantage, my friend and I parted company with most of the fish we hooked from shore. In the majority of cases the tarpon simply shook the fly free in a series of contorted head gyrations that snapped like the whip cars in the amusement parks of yesteryear. In one episode, the tippet became fouled in a floating log and it broke before I could free it. At least there were no knot failures but after about two hours of furious fishing I realized I only had two remaining leaders in my shirt pocket. My friend was in worse shape. After losing his last fish he came running to me and started yelling that he needed another leader. I told him, "No way. I have two left and I'm going to use them." I think he would have exhibited less disbelief and agony if he received news that he would have to repeat one of his classes. Not sure of what he just heard, he asked, "Are you serious?" I replied that I was dead serious. I directed him to my tackle bag where I stored my leader material and informed him that if he wanted to continue fishing he would have to tie his own leaders. I'll never forget the sight of him seated in the sand fumbling and yelling obscenities as he tried to tie his first Bimini twist. Attempting this knot for the first time can be a little intimidating. Imagine trying to get it right when giant tarpon are rolling right in front of you. My friend finally put together something that looked like a tangled length of linguini stuck to a pot. I guess it was just as well because he didn't hook another fish before it was time to leave. I went back to the lodge with my two leaders intact and told him that they were two less that I had to tie for the next day's fishing. That evening the young lady found herself stuck with the company of her dad.

Personally, I like tying knots and am always on the lookout to learn new ones that are applicable to fly-fishing. It would probably take volumes to discuss and illustrate all the knots developed over the years for commercial and sportfishing purposes, but fortunately we don't have to involve ourselves is such a monumental undertaking. If you are like me, you might derive a lot of satisfaction just from knowing how to tie a large assortment of knots. However, that isn't necessary for most fly-fishing situations you are likely to encounter. There are a few proven connections that are vital to the fly-fishing mode and these are the ones I will focus on. One mark of an accomplished angler is knowing how to tie the right knot for any given situation.

In any discussion of knots, the primary consideration is *knot strength*. Knot strength is the breaking strength of

a line which has a knot tied in it. Many anglers, especially those who are new to the sport, do not realize that most knots actually weaken a line. Basically a knot involves a section of line going back on itself or on another section of line in a series of turns, twists or bends. This interlacing of sections can cause one segment to cut into another segment, weakening the integrity of that particular section of line. The object here is to avoid knots that significantly

A Rhode Island bluefish.

weaken a line. For example, one of the first knots you probably learned how to tie as a kid is a simple overhand knot. This is sometimes referred to as a cutting knot, because in the process of being tightened, that is exactly the effect it has on the line. Depending on the line manufacturer, the rated breaking strength can be reduced by as much as 50%.

Knot strength is expressed as a percentage of the breaking capacity of unknotted line. In this chapter I'm going to present some data compiled by Dave Justice of Sufix lines regarding the breaking strength of the knots that I will be discussing. Sufix manufactures some great

Bimini Twist

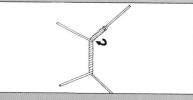

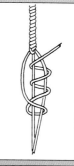

1. Take the tag end of the line and bring it back to the standing part so that you have a loop that is approximately 2 feet long. Put your left hand inside the loop (reverse this if you are left-handed) and rotate your hand 20 times, forming a series of twists.

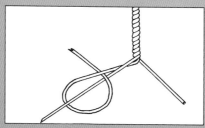

4. By maintaining the tag end at a right angle and simultaneously pulling up on the standing part while pushing up at the "V", a series of neat barrel wraps will form over the column.

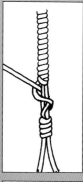

6. Now that the half hitch has secured the wraps, you can remove the loop from your knee. Take the tag end and make 4 or 5 turns over both strands of the loop working back toward the column of barrel wraps.

2. Slip the loop over your knee and spread both hands apart. This will cause the column of twists to tighten.

3. Work your hands down to the point where you can place the index finger of your left hand at the "V" formed at the bottom of the juncture of the column of twists. With your left hand, position the tag end so it is at a right angle to the column of twists. Pulling slightly upward on the standing part of the line and simultaneously applying upward pressure with your index finger, will cause the tag end to roll over the column of twists. It is important to make this first roll over (sometimes you can hear a slight click as the tag end first crosses over).

5. When the tag end has wrapped over the entire column, slide your right hand down the column and pinch the "V" together between your thumb and index finger. With your left hand, take a half hitch with the tag end around the left leg of the loop and pull it up tight.

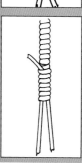

7. Pull the tag end slowly so that the spirals begin to tighten. To make these spirals tighten uniformly against the column of barrel wraps, it may be necessary to tease out slack by pushing back on the spirals and then pulling the tag end in the opposite direction.

8. With everything snugged down tight, trim the tag end leaving about a 1/8-inch nub.

---

lines that I highly recommend for tippet material. They also have some very sophisticated testing equipment, so the data that Dave provided me is very accurate. If you tie these knots correctly, you should attain some of these break strengths. However, regardless of the particular knot you are tying, one point to bear in mind is that the knot must be drawn up properly to attain its full potential. Knots that are not completely tightened may slip under pressure, and a knot that slips will eventually break. To help avoid this, in the process of drawing up a knot, lubricate it with saliva. This reduces friction and makes the knot easier to tighten.

The Bimini Twist

For most people, the Bimini twist is the most intimidating of all knots. It is probably the one knot that will require the most practice because you have to develop a feel to get the line to roll over itself when making the barrel wraps. But do not be put off. I have taught hundreds of

people how to tie it and with a little practice and patience you will soon master it. But is this knot absolutely necessary for most saltwater applications? More than likely, it's not. For most inshore encounters you can get by without it, but there is no denying the fact that it is the best knot you can tie for a variety of applications. When I am only using a single length of tippet material that will be connected to the end of the fly line, I often use the Bimini because it affords the strongest connection. The resulting loop which is twisted and doubled over itself also serves as a good substitute for a heavier butt section which can be simply eliminated. And in those cases when I need a heavy monofilament shock tippet, the Bimini loop in the lighter class tippet forms the basis for the connection with the large-diameter shock leader.

So how strong is the Bimini? Dave answered this very convincingly. Working with a line sample that had an average breaking strain of 26.66 pounds (the high was

Trilene Knot

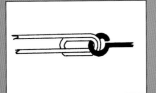   

1. Pass the tag end of the line through the hook eye twice forming a small, double-strand loop.

2. Spiral the tag end around the standing part of the line 5 or 6 times and then pass it through the double strand loop.

3. Begin to tighten the wraps by alternately pulling on the tag end and standing part of the line. When the wraps are fairly snug, finish tightening the knot by pulling on the standing part.

Finished knot.

27.79 and the low was 25.40), Dave found that a 20-turn Bimini broke at 27.79-pound test, the highest figure that was obtained for the original unknotted line. You can't get any better than that. By comparison, the spider hitch, which some anglers will tell you is just as good as the Bimini, tested at 20.03 pounds breaking strength. In a fishing situation, that can amount to a significant difference. I look at it this way. You will spend time and money to go fishing, even when you make local outings. When the moment of truth arrives and you have a fish on, the line becomes the critical connection between you and your quarry. It only makes sense then to try and use knots that do not significantly weaken the line's unknotted breaking strength. Refer to the illustrations for tying instructions.

The Trilene Knot

This is one of the best knots for tying a fly snug against a class tippet. It is a variation of the popular clinch knot, but here a double turn is taken through the hook eye which accounts for this knot's near 100% breaking strength.

The Non-Slip Mono Loop

At times you may want to maximize a fly's action so instead of snugging it up tight against the leader, a loop knot is used to allow the fly to swing freely. For a long time I used the 5-turn surgeon's knot favored by famed Florida Keys guide, Steve Huff. However, Dave's tests proved that the non-slip mono knot is actually stronger. When tied in a line with an average unknotted breaking strength of 23.61 pounds, the non-slip mono knot yielded a break strength of 21.61 pounds. That's 92% knot strength. The best the 5-turn surgeon's yielded was 81% knot strength. The non-slip mono loop knot is tied as follows.

Non-Slip Mono Loop

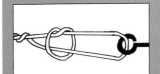

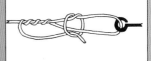

1. Form an overhand knot approximately 6 inches from the tag end of the line. Then pass the tag end through the hook eye and back through the center of the overhand knot.

2. Take a series of turns around the standing part of the line. The number of turns you take depends on the breaking strength of the line you are using. For 8- to 12-pound-test lines, make 5 turns, with lines testing 15 to 40 pounds, take 4 turns. If

you are using a heavy shock tippet of 50-pound test or more, all you need is 3 turns.

3. After making the wraps, pass the tag end back through the overhand knot, making sure it re-enters from the same side it exited. Begin snugging up the wraps by slowly pulling on the tag end.

4. Grasp the standing part of the line in one hand, and the hook or fly in the other hand. For safety's sake, you may want to secure the hook with pliers. Pull your hands apart and the knot will tighten.

Surgeon's Loop

This is one of the easiest ways to fasten an end loop in a leader. When I use a butt section, I tie this knot to have a loop-to-loop connection with the fly line.

I also use this knot to form end loops in lead-core line and mono running lines. First, you have to extract about 5 inches of lead filament from the braid. This is accomplished by alternately pushing down on the outer braid and gently pulling out the lead core. Break off the filament. Then fold the core-less braid back over itself to

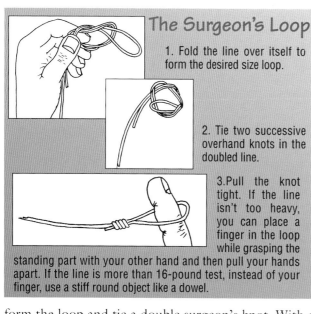

The Surgeon's Loop

1. Fold the line over itself to form the desired size loop.

2. Tie two successive overhand knots in the doubled line.

3. Pull the knot tight. If the line isn't too heavy, you can place a finger in the loop while grasping the standing part with your other hand and then pull your hands apart. If the line is more than 16-pound test, instead of your finger, use a stiff round object like a dowel.

Uni-Knot

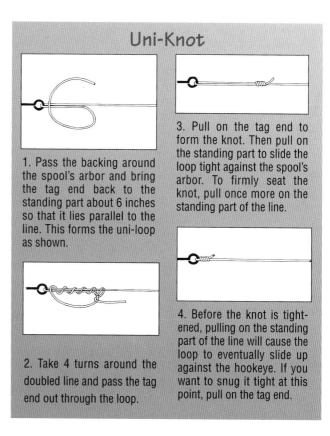

1. Pass the backing around the spool's arbor and bring the tag end back to the standing part about 6 inches so that it lies parallel to the line. This forms the uni-loop as shown.

2. Take 4 turns around the doubled line and pass the tag end out through the loop.

3. Pull on the tag end to form the knot. Then pull on the standing part to slide the loop tight against the spool's arbor. To firmly seat the knot, pull once more on the standing part of the line.

4. Before the knot is tightened, pulling on the standing part of the line will cause the loop to eventually slide up against the hookeye. If you want to snug it tight at this point, pull on the tag end.

form the loop and tie a double surgeon's knot. With a mono running line all you have to do is fold the line over itself and form the desired loop and tie the surgeon's knot. I make the front loop on the running line about 4 inches long. This makes it possible to pass a coiled shooting head through the loop. Now you can change shooting heads in less than a minute. The loop at the other end of the running line is about a 1/4 inch. This is interlocked with the Bimini loop that is tied in the backing.

Uni-Knot

The uni-knot can also be used to fasten an end loop in the leader but I prefer the non-slip mono loop knot. Instead, because it can be slid into place before it is tightened, I use the uni-knot for tying the backing to spool's arbor.

Speed Nail Knot Shock Tippet Connection

When I fish more distant locales outside my home waters, the conditions and species frequently call for the use of a large-diameter shock tippet. Tarpon fishing is a good example. Their abrasive jaw can quickly wear through a class tippet. In fact, anytime you confront species or conditions that are likely to saw through a small-diameter tippet, you should consider tying on a shock or bite leader. If you are record conscious, the length of the unknotted class tippet must be a minimum of 15 inches measured between the knots. The shock leader, be it heavy mono or wire, cannot exceed 12 inches and that is measured from outside the knots used to make the connection.

One of the best methods of connecting a mono shock tippet to the class tippet's Bimini loop is by means of a nail knot tied in the heavy leader. It is referred to as a speed nail knot because you don't need a hollow tube to tie it. All you need is a stiff, round, fairly small-diameter object like a needle, toothpick or a length of wire. I make it a practice to try and have all my leaders tied in advance before I ever hit the fishing grounds. In most cases you'll find this a lot more practical than trying to tie knots from a pitching boat deck, or in the case of my hapless former student, sprawled out on the sand with schools of tarpon rolling in front of you.

The speed nail knot shock tippet connection.

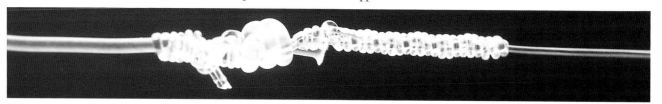

Speed Nail Knot

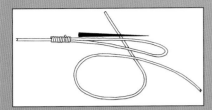

1. Place a needle or similar object alongside the end portion of the class tippet's Bimini loop. Form about a 6-inch loop in the shock leader, lay it under the needle and Bimini loop, and pinch everything together between the thumb and index finger of your left hand.

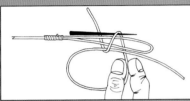

2. With your right hand, take the right leg of the shock leader loop and wrap it over everything, the needle, the Bimini loop, and the standing part of the leader itself.

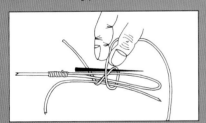

3. Take about 3 wraps working to the left.

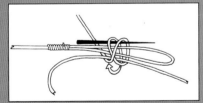

4. Pinch the wraps together with your left hand and begin tightening the knot by pulling on the right tag end of the leader. Then begin pulling the left tag end of the leader. Do not make it too tight because you have to pull the needle out.

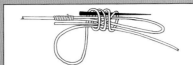

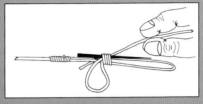

5. Grasp the nail knot with your left hand and pull the Bimini loop with your right hand. This will cause the Bimini knot to snug up tight against the nail knot. Finish tightening the nail knot by pulling simultaneously on both tag ends in opposite directions. Because you will be working with large-diameter mono, to tighten it properly, it helps to secure at least one of the tag ends with pliers.

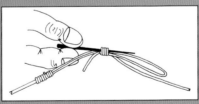

6. Make 3 successive half hitches around the shock leader with the Bimini loop, snugging up each one tightly as you proceed.

7. Slip the needle out from under the wraps while holding the nail knot and Bimini firmly in place with your right hand. This will prevent the Bimini loop from slipping out through the shock leader wraps.

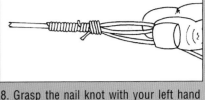

8. Grasp the nail knot with your left hand and pull on the Bimini loop with your right hand to snug the Bimini knot against the nail knot. Finish tightening the nail knot by pulling on both ends of the shock leader. To seat these wraps as tightly as possible, it helps to grab one end of the shock leader with pliers.

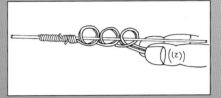

9. Make 3 separate half hitches around the shock leader with the Bimini loop and snug each one up tightly.

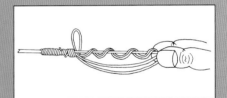

10. Take the remaining Bimini loop and spiral it around the shock leader 4 times.

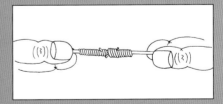

11. Snug these wraps tight against the half hitches. Trim the remaining end of the Bimini loop and the left tag end of the shock leader and the connection is complete.

However, for those times when you're caught short and have to tie leaders when you're out fishing, I carry a little tool to tie the speed nail knot. It's a simple saltwater-size snap swivel. Unfasten the snap and bend it so it lies straight. Now you have a small length of wire that you can wrap the mono around to tie the nail knot. The ring on the other end makes it convenient to tie the snap to a fishing vest or jacket. That way the tool is always within easy reach.

To visualize how this knot works, fold your hand over the extended index finger of the other hand, making a fist-like grip. This is how the heavy mono

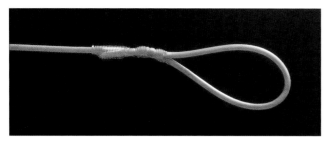

An end loop fastened in a fly line using speed nail knots tied with 10-pound-test monofilament.

enfolds the lighter line. It's quite simple to tie. As mentioned in Chapter 2, I also use the speed nail knot to fasten end loops in the fly line. When making fly line end loops instead of tying a nail knot with heavy leader material, I use light mono like 8- or 10-pound test. This small-diameter mono bites into the folded section of the fly line securing a loop that is as strong as the fly line itself. For the fly line loop, tie two separate 6- to 7-turn nail knots about an 1/8 of an inch apart. However, for the shock tippet connection, instead of doubled over fly line, you are wrapping over the class tippet's Bimini loop. And since you will be using heavy, large-diameter mono, you only need to make 3 complete turns.

Speed Nail Knot
Tippet to Tippet Connection

A very effective way to connect tippet sections that may differ considerably in breaking strength and diameter is to use the speed nail connection described above. The only difference is omitting the Bimini in the lighter section of line. Instead of tying the Bimini to form the double line, simply fold about 10 inches of the lighter line over itself and tie the speed nail knot in the heavier section of line you want to connect it to. This is one of my favorite connections for tying striped bass leaders. Typically I have a three- to five-foot length of a 40- to 50-pound butt section that I want to connect to a tippet in the 12- to 16-pound-test range. Tying a Bimini in the light line would make for a rather bulky connection. To avoid this I double a portion of the 12- or 16-pound test and connect it to the butt section using the speed nail knot method for the heavier line. Once again, Dave's tests at Suffix proved that this makes for a very strong connection, 91.9% breaking strength to be exact. You don't get the 100% you would with the Bimini, but the tradeoff is that you save a little time by not having to tie the Bimini knot.

Like most fly-fishers, for years I used the blood knot to make these connections, but I prefer the speed nail knot method. The standard blood knot works best with lines that are of similar diameter. But as I'll explain in the next section, you have to be careful to make the required number of turns when wrapping one line around the other. Secondly, when you want to connect lines that differ considerably in diameter, with the blood knot you will have to double the lighter line and reduce the number of wraps you make with the heavier line. Not only is this improved version of the blood knot more difficult to tie, you also have to be sure to draw the two sections of the knot up properly. If the two lines are not firmly seated together, the breaking strength will be reduced to as little as 60% of the rated strength of the lighter line.

Blood Knot

When tying this knot to join lines that are fairly uniform in diameter it is very important to make at least 6 spiral wraps around each standing part of the lines you are joining. Referring again to Dave Justice's data, he found that a 5-turn knot only yielded 60% breaking strength whereas a 6-turn knot resulted in 90% knot strength. Here is how you tie it:

Blood Knot

1. Overlap the two lines you want to join together, allowing about 8 inches of each tag end to protrude on either side. This length will leave enough room to make the required number of wraps. Spiral one tag end around the standing part of the other line, taking a minimum of 6 turns. Then take that tag end, bend it back over the spirals, and push it **down** between the two strands of line.

2. Take the other tag end and repeat Step 1, twisting it around the other part and bringing it back through the center loop. This time however, the tag end should be pushed **up** through the center loop.

3. If you have proceeded correctly up to this point, this is how the knot should look at this stage.

4. This is one knot that requires particular care in the tightening process. Pull up alternately on both tag ends and both standing parts to take most of the slack.

5. Continue tightening until the spirals begin to form barrel wraps.

6. Complete the tightening process by pulling on the standing parts in opposite directions.

*Mark the fly line's designated weight class with hash marks (these equal 5)
and dashes (a single dash equals 1). This line is an 8-weight.*

Haywire Twist

There are occasions when even a heavy mono shock leader will not prevent you from getting bit off. Sharks, wahoo, king mackerel, big bluefish and barracuda are leading examples of species that nature equipped with a mean set of dentures. In cases like these, you'll have to resort to wire. However, be advised that there are times when some of these fish can get leader shy and they will often refuse a fly with a wire trace. This is particularly the case with Pacific barracuda.

I discovered this in my early baitfishing days when it was possible to catch big barracuda right off the piers in Southern California. You could nail them on feathered lead-head jig or if you had the money, live anchovies were the preferred offerings, but there were many times when the folks using wire were hard-pressed to draw strikes. If you tied the bait hook to a mono leader, the cudas would respond but you also lost a good many hooks and fish in the process. Years later I faced the same dilemma fly-fishing for barracuda in Southern California. The barracuda there readily responded to flies. But if you attached wire, oftentimes you found that you ended up with steady refusals. It can be a tough trade-off.

The same dilemma can also apply to fishing wahoo, but my opportunity to connect with these awesome speedsters is so limited that I never forego the use of wire. I recommend single-strand wire over braided multi-strand because for any given pound test it is smaller in diameter and you don't need any crimps to secure it. Rather than tie the wire directly to the class tippet, I tie a small, black swivel to the tag end of the tippet. Then I use a haywire twist to connect one end of the wire to the

swivel and the other end to the fly. As long as the wire and swivel combination does not exceed 12 inches, this setup conforms to IGFA specifications. While casting with a 12-inch mono shock leader doesn't pose a problem, a similar length of wire would prevent the fly from turning over properly. So, as a general rule, your wire leaders shouldn't be more than about 5 inches long. The key to getting a strong connection with the haywire twist is to make true "X's" when criss-crossing the wire. If you merely spiral the tag end around the standing part, under pressure the wraps may unravel.

On the second long-range trip devoted exclusively to fly-fishing that Ed Rice put together we were lucky to hit some really hot wahoo fishing. If you were fortunate to have a fly in the water when the wahoo came racing through to attack the live anchovies being used as chum, you got bit. It was that simple. The only trouble was that a few guys missed the opportunity of a lifetime because they either didn't have a wire leader, or in at least two cases I know of, the leader wasn't properly tied. I was the only one onboard who had small black swivels and by the time I finished rigging up a few of my buddies, there were none left for yours truly. As it turned out, it really didn't matter because when my slot was open to fish the stern of the boat the "hoos" had moved on. The haywire twist is tied as follows:

Haywire Twist

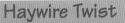

1. Bend the tag end of the wire against the standing part forming a loop. If you don't have strong fingers, grasp the end of the loop with pliers. With the end portion of the loop firmly secured, begin criss-crossing the wire with the tag end. Twist both sections of wire simultaneously to form true "X's."

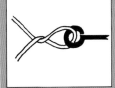

2. Make a minimum of 3 "X's."

3. Bend the tag end of the wire at a right angle to the standing part and make 4-barrel wraps around the standing part.

4. Do not cut the tag end of the wire because it will leave a sharp edge that can cause injury. Instead, bend the tag end to form a makeshift handle. Then bend this handle opposite the direction of the wraps and the wire should break off cleanly. If it didn't break on the first try, rotate the handle back and forth until the wire finally breaks.

CHAPTER 4

The Ultimate Deception: Saltwater Flies

We're all familiar with expressions like, "you can't judge a book by its cover," or "looks can be deceiving." If you think about it, these folk sayings are especially applicable to the realm of sport fishing because as anglers we're engaged in the art of deception. If you are using some kind of natural bait, the ruse lies in the fact that the edible morsel comes with a hook attached. Something the fish didn't bargain for. There was a student film shot years ago that puts an interesting twist on this age-old trick. I don't recall all the particulars but the scene goes something this: A fellow is surf fishing early in the morning and happens upon what appears to be a brown paper lunch bag sitting on the beach. The fisherman looks around, doesn't see anyone about, so he bends down, picks up the bag, opens it and pulls out a delicious looking sandwich. He takes a bite and the next thing you see is the guy struggling at the end of a line as he's being pulled into the water. I remember having mixed reactions to it at the time. I thought it was funny and I started laughing, but I also found it a bit eerie. I don't know if the young film maker intended it as an anti-fishing piece. It certainly didn't have that effect on me, or other anglers I know who have seen it. But I think about it sometimes when I'm trying to get a fish to eat something that I'm offering.

As fly-fishers who use only artificial offerings to entice fish, we take this con game one step further than our bait-fishermen counterparts. What we are presenting to the fish is fake. It isn't even the real thing, but we're trying to get the fish to react to it by striking it and we want it to strike with its mouth, not by means of some other body part like a tail. This may seem obvious but it brings to mind the one and only encounter I've ever had with a thresher shark on fly tackle.

A striper taken on a Bob's Banger.

Years ago in Southern California there was a good population of thresher sharks, but sadly like other facets of this fishery, it drastically declined when the Fish and Game Commission allowed drift gillnetting. Anyway, in the early 70s I was lucky enough to at least enjoy some of this great fishing just before its demise, but all my encounters with this magnificent shark were on big-game, conventional tackle. But even with 80-pound-class outfits, I never felt I was overgunned with any of the threshers I hooked. In terms of all-out staying power, these sharks can hold their own with practically anything that swims. It's their tail fins that give them their incredible pulling power. Nature intended these fins to aid in the feeding process, so unlike other sharks with well-developed tail fins, the ones on threshers are more extreme versions that can actually exceed their entire body length. Compared to other species of shark, the mouth on a thresher is relatively small for its size and its teeth, while no doubt effective, seem nowhere near as formidable as the dentures you find on makos or tiger sharks. But if you are ever privileged to see threshers actively feeding, you'll understand that their tails more than compensate for any shortcomings they may have in this regard.

When they're available, mackerel are one of their favorite food sources and threshers use their enormous tails to corral the school into tight balls where they whack them with broad sweeps of their fin. The stunned mackerel aren't going anywhere fast so the thresher can methodically pick them off one by one. They don't need bucket-size mouths because they're not tearing into schools headfirst.

On one of my first charter trips off Ensenada, Mexico, I stood on the boat's bridge next to the captain to get a better view of a thresher herding a school of sardines on the surface. The skipper spoke good English and jokingly drew an analogy to his own style of eating where he used tortillas to compact a serving of beans and rice. Years later when I was fly-fishing sharks from my skiff, I was totally surprised when a thresher appeared in the chum slick. To my knowledge no one has ever taken a thresher on fly and here was my one and only chance. The creation I had on couldn't even be rightly called a pattern. It was simply pieces of red marabou wound palmer style around a 3/0 hook. My intention was to simulate the quarter-size pieces of mackerel and bonito

that made up part of my chum slick. It worked very well on blue sharks but the thresher was a little more discriminating. As the shark started swimming in the direction of the fly, my buddy onboard started shouting, "he's going to take it." I really thought so too, but something in that creature's primitive brain triggered a response I hadn't anticipated. It swam toward the fly for several yards and then abruptly veered off smacking it with its tail. My friend is the consummate optimist and this time he shouted, "he'll come back and eat it." It didn't happen.

CAPTAIN JOE BLADOS

There's no doubt that flies represent the one component in our tackle system where you are confronted with the greatest variety of choices. Recommendations abound. Usually all it takes is a chat with someone who ties their own and in no time you're likely to be flooded with suggestions as to what works best for a particular species. Even for specific regions like Southern California, the Gulf Coast, Baja, the Florida Keys or Martha's Vineyard, the seemingly endless array of patterns to choose from can be a bit overwhelming. Of course, I would be one of the first to agree that a good deal of the fun of fly-fishing involves trying out new creations to see what will work under a given set of conditions. But so many times someone ties a fly where all they've done is make some

Jeff Solis with something to crow about, a roosterfish from the beach.

minor changes to a basic pattern, the fly catches them fish, and the first thing they do is give it a new name. In some cases this smacks of plagiarism. Anyone who has created a new pattern like Lefty Kreh's Deceiver, Bob Clouser's Clouser Minnow, Bob Popovics' Surf Candy or Dan Blanton's Whistler, has experienced instances where their pattern has been appropriated by someone who's tied it slightly differently and then goes on to tout it as their new pattern. Dishonesty aside, all this does is add to the confusion. At least with my limited fly-tying ability, I don't have to worry about someone ripping me off. A second advantage that accrues when you tie flies as poorly as I do is that you don't have to give any away because no one ever asks you for one. I've been at tackle shows with Bob Popovics where he's tied dozens of flies over the weekend only to return home empty handed. I tied once at a show and the few that I left on the table were gone the next morning. Secretly I felt pretty good that someone thought enough of my creations to make off with them. That ended when I found out that the night janitor thought they were part of the trash left lying around and he swept them away with the rest of the junk.

Realizing that we are trying to entice fish with something that is totally artificial, I guess it's only natural to have concerns about how the fly will be received by the fish. Do they think it looks appetizing? Does it appear edible? Of course, the only conclusive answer comes from the fish itself. But there are fly-fishers like myself who seek some advance assurance in this very uncertain game. We would like to have some idea beforehand as to how effective our particular fly is likely to be. I draw criticism from some of my friends for my habit of asking others what they think of the fly. I'm not looking for compliments. I know better. A friend accompanied me on a trip to Baja a few years ago and he would chuckle whenever I asked the captain if he thought my fly looked good in the water. This guy figured that because the captain didn't want to offend me and possibly risk getting a miserly tip, he would always give a positive answer. What he didn't realize was that the captain and I were friends and that I fished with him on many of my trips to Baja. This skipper fished these waters all his life and despite all the time I had put in over the years, I knew this was no substitute for his intimate, local knowledge. Besides, if this skipper thought the fly wasn't appropriate for a given set of conditions, he would not hesitate in telling me so. To the untrained eye, or to someone unfamiliar with the locale, a given fly may look good, but that doesn't have anything to do with whether or not the fish will find it to their liking.

In partial defense of my humble fly-tying ability, let me say that my goal is to try and construct flies that will catch fish, not fishermen. Anyone who has put considerable time in this sport knows that there are all kinds of creations on the market that are intended to catch anglers first and maybe fish second. What we sometimes overlook is the fact that what appeals to us may not have the same effect on the fish. One of the most perfect sand crab imitations I have ever seen was a rubber crab that was designed for use by spin-fishermen. I know some truly talented fly-tiers and none of them could ever make such a convincing replica. I also don't know of anyone who ever caught anything on one of these crabs. It's no wonder you don't find them in the tackle stores anymore. I'm sure that whoever manufactured them was positive that fish like barred surf perch, corbina and yellowfin croaker that actively feed on sand crabs, would find this authentic-looking rubber creation to their liking. I bought six of them. It wasn't a lot of money but it was money that was wasted.

The point of all this for any of you who would like to start tying your own flies, is that saltwater patterns do have to come off as artistic masterpieces. It is far more important to strive for a reasonably good imitation of the fish's principal food sources. For example, in much of the coastal U.S., anchovies, mackerel, sardines and rainfish are the primary baitfish. All of these bait have dark-colored backs in hues that vary from shades of green to blue/black. There is usually some silver coloration on their sides and their bellies are white. In terms of color alone, if you tie patterns with these combinations, you more than likely will have a fly that fish feeding on these baitfish will strike.

Regardless of the pattern you are trying to tie, there are three relevant factors that should be taken into consideration: the fly's fish appeal, its castability and its durability. A fly's fish appeal will be largely a function of its length, shape and color. For example, if you want to fish for yellowtail in Southern California or Baja, and you know that they are feeding primarily on six-inch "Tinker" mackerel, you will stand a good chance of drawing strikes if you present a fly that simulates the mackerel's size and color. You do not have to strive to tie an exact imitation. But the fly's appearance is only one concern. What you also have to consider is the fly's sink rate. Even if the fly looks good, it has to get to where the fish are feeding. This will largely depend on the type of fly line used (floating, sinking), but it is also a function of the type of fly and how it is tied. When fish are feeding fairly deep in the water column, as is often the case with yellowtail, you have to get the fly down as quickly as possible. But if the fly is tied with naturally buoyant materials such as deer hair with nothing like dumbbell eyes or wraps of lead wire to help it sink, its effectiveness will be compromised.

Two instances stand out in my mind where I had beautifully tied flies from two very talented tiers but they didn't do the job because they did not sink properly. One was a squid pattern tied by a young fellow from San Francisco (I don't want to mention names where I think the person might be unnecessarily embarrassed) that I met one year at the San Mateo show. He heard that I was looking for some squid flies for yellowtail fishing and offered to tie me a few. They were some of the most realistic squid patterns I have ever seen. I was showing them to some friends in an Italian restaurant one night, and when the waiter saw them, he asked if we wanted them cooked for appetizers. On a trip to the Coronado Islands a few weeks afterward, this was the first fly I tied on. The yellowtail were feeding on squid and I figured that this fly would be the perfect offering. The only problem was that the yellows were taking the squid about 30 feet below the surface and this fly floated like a lobster-pot buoy. I should have known from the start that it wouldn't sink because it was tied on a length of 1/8-inch-diameter plastic tubing, a very buoyant material, but it looked so convincing that I totally overlooked that fact.

Three thousand miles away on a shallow-water flat off the east end of Long Island, I find myself similarly frustrated with a beautifully tied crab pattern that simply takes too long to slip below the surface. There are times when a slow-sinking crab imitation can be effective but this wasn't one of them. The water depth off Gardiner's Island where I was fishing was only about five feet, but there was a fairly strong current and the stripers seemed strictly oriented to feeding off the bottom. A crab slipping ever so slowly beneath the surface didn't seem natural and the bass ignored it like it was a broken piece of clamshell.

Related to sink rate is the ease with which you can cast the fly. You can have a great-looking pattern, but it isn't worth much if you can't get it out to the fish. Of course, one's casting ability is a primary consideration here. As we'll see in Chapter 5, casting skill is the key element in this sport, and regardless of the pattern, if you can't effectively cast a line, the fly isn't going anywhere. This said, there is no denying the fact that some patterns are easier to cast than others and this is something to be aware of when choosing or tying flies. Large, bulky patterns are going to offer more wind resistance and in that respect they will be more difficult to cast than sleeker patterns. Big-game patterns like those designed for billfish can take on the proportions of a feather duster and they can be about as unwieldy to cast. Fortunately, under most circumstances where flies this size come into play, the fish are teased close to the boat and long casts aren't necessary. Heavily-weighted flies upset the dynamics of the fly line and it will take practice to get used to casting them. The point is, the patterns that are easiest to cast are not always the ones you want to be fishing with.

I don't know of any fly-fisher who wouldn't gladly sacrifice a fly in the interests of catching a fish. Having your prized creation mauled beyond recognition by a predator game fish bent on devouring it is something most of us look forward to and hope for. But if, after repeated casting, it starts to shed material like sheep at shearing time, the fly is definitely not tied properly. The locale and species you fish for will certainly affect a fly's longevity. Tooth-studded predators like barracuda, bluefish and sharks can cost you a lot of flies. In fact, when I fish sharks, I usually don't even try and retrieve the fly. It's a lot safer to just cut the wire leader and forget about the fly. Fishing an environment like the surf can also take its toll. The turbulence of the water and the abrasive effect of sand and rocks can dull hooks, dislodge eyes and rip off feathers. I recall a sand crab pattern that was tied with folded stands of bucktail. The bucktail was intended to simulate the crab's shell. But even when it was coated with head cement, the strands of bucktail inevitably would break and the fly ended up looking more like a punk rock hairpiece than a sand crab. Finishing off flies with epoxy coatings adds to their durability, but when you're fishing tough species in bad neighborhoods, you have to expect a certain amount of loss. If I return from a trip with all the flies I started out with, it's usually an indication that the fishing wasn't very good.

Almost everywhere you turn these days there is a new fly pattern that someone is either writing about or trying to market. I'm sure that at one time or another they will all interest fish, but this can make the selection process all the more difficult. To give you a sense of perspective and make your choices a little easier, I'm going to limit my discussion to seven different patterns that have consistently produced for me everywhere I've fished. Obviously to adjust for local conditions, modifications may have to be made taking into account factors like appropriate hook sizes, length of materials, color combinations and whether or not the fly should be weighted. But the beauty of these patterns is that their

basic design has proven to be consistently effective on a wide variety of game fish under just about any condition imaginable.

For those who do not tie, the patterns I'm about to discuss can be purchased through most major fly shops. Two very talented tiers I can highly recommend are Frank Abbate (Island Saltwater Flies, P.O. Box 5352, Hauppauge, N.Y. 11788, e-mail isalwatfly@aol.com) and Glen Mikkleson (Atlantic Flies, 516•878•0883). These two gentlemen do this for a living and I can personally attest to the quality of their flies. Due to the volume of their business, if you're planning to place an order, give them a couple of months lead time. Another great source of innovative flies and fly-tying material is Enrico Puglisi Ltd. (55 West Hills Road, Huntington Station, NY 11746.)

Tying your own flies is a wonderful hobby in itself as evidenced by the fact that there are people who tie but seldom, if ever, fish. For many diehard anglers, it's the next best thing to being out on the water and can help fill the void for those times when you can't go fishing. The ultimate satisfaction of course, is actually catching fish on a fly you made yourself. Maybe this has something to do with a primordial urge programmed into our genes eons ago when the ability to use one's hands to fashion basic implements was literally a life-or-death proposition. That is seldom the case today in our world of pre-packaged and mass-produced goods where it's increasingly difficult to directly experience the fruits of one's labors. But tying one's own flies and catching fish with them is a truly authentic experience. It represents a victory in a personal contest with nature, and for many people that is a refreshingly different experience.

Of course to tie flies you will need tools, and if you are really handy and have the time, you can fashion your own. In the early seventies when I moved back to Southern California, I bought two fly-tying vises that were made from the jaws of pliers. I forget who originally came up with this idea, but it was a clever bit of engineering, and they worked. I still have mine but I value them more as collector's items and conversation pieces. Another innovative creation that modified a common, everyday tool into a useful tying instrument involved the use of vise grips. Here the engineering was a lot simpler than that required with the pliers' jaws because the only change that had to be made was welding a length of metal bar to one of the handles so it could be used in conjunction with a clamp. I think Bill Barnes still has a pair of these affixed to the fly-tying bench at his lodge, Casa Mar.

I think the ultimate evolution in fly-tying vises is the original rotary vise designed by Andy Renzetti. Like Ted Juracsik, Andy is also a gifted machinist with a love for fly-fishing and it shows in all his products from his fly-tying bobbins to his vises. As testimony to the old adage that imitation is the best form of flattery, Andy's vise has been copied more than any other. So, do you need a vise of this caliber to tie good flies? Of course not. But even for a butcher like myself, the fact that it holds hooks with the authority of a pit bull clamping down on a bone, coupled with its true rotary design, makes the job a whole lot easier. It's also the vise of choice for luminaries like Lefty, Clouser and Popovics, and these guys are considerably more skilled at this than I am. As you can see, imitation takes many forms.

The Lefty's Deceiver

I guess it's only appropriate to begin this section with a discussion of the most popular saltwater pattern of all time. Lefty originated the fly in the late 1950s (he couldn't tell me the exact year) primarily for striped bass in Chesapeake Bay, but the Deceiver has proven itself in waters the world over, both fresh and salt. The reason the pattern has earned universal recognition is simply because it works so well and it's easy to understand why. The Deceiver incorporates all the qualities you look for in a well-designed pattern. It has a shape that closely resembles the profile of most baitfish, so larger predators are readily attracted to it. This profile makes it easy to cast even when tied in relatively long lengths, and if the materials are tied in correctly, the fly will not foul. I have a special fondness for the Deceiver, because it is the first fly that my buddy John Posh taught me to tie and I took my very first striper with it that same afternoon in John's home waters at the mouth of the Housatonic River in Connecticut. I've tied hundreds of Deceivers since then in varying sizes and colors and have taken fish with the pattern practically everywhere I've wet a line. If there were ever a universal saltwater pattern, the Deceiver would be it.

Tying the Deceiver

Hooks: As is the case with the other patterns I will discuss, hook sizes are partly a function of the size of the fly you want to tie. Generally for inshore species, hook sizes can range from 1s to 3/0s. The Mustad 34007 and Tiemco 800S are two of my favorites.

Tail Section: A minimum of six (three on each side) wide saddle or neck hackles are tied in at the rear portion of the hook for a tail section in such a manner

The author's modified Deceiver pattern, designated the Sardina.

that the feathers flare inward. To get the feathers to lay together properly, form each pair separately. Lay the feathers one on top of the other, and then dip each pair in the water separately. Then lay both pairs together and wet them all again. Now you can tie all the feathers in at one time. If you want some flash, you can tie in 6 to 10 strands of Krystal Flash or Flashabou.

Collar: With the feathers tied in, wind the thread to approximately 1/4 inch behind the hook eye and tie in either bucktail or calf tail for a collar. Lefty recommends tying it in two stages, one bunch on the near side of the hook, the second bunch on the far side of the hook. Make sure the collar extends beyond the hook bend. I normally do not bother (maybe that's why my flies look the way they do), but you can simulate gills by tying in about a dozen strands of red Flashabou or Krystal Flash on the underside of the fly behind the hook eye.

Topping: To simulate the dark-colored backs normally found on most baitfish, you can tie in a few strands of peacock herl on top of the fly immediately behind the hook eye. This material should extend back about three-quarters of the length of the fly.

Eyes: The first few years when I was tying and fishing the Deceiver, I never added any eyes, but along with Lefty, I feel that they should be part of the fly. Baitfish tend to have comparatively large eyes. When you're trying to survive in an environment where many of your co-inhabitants are determined to make a meal of you, good vision is literally a lifesaver. So maybe to even things out a bit in their eat-or-be-eaten world, nature equipped most baitfish with a good pair of eyes. I haven't kept records, but I feel that the addition of eyes to my patterns has enhanced their effectiveness. It makes

A striper fooled by a Clouser Minnow.

the fly look more realistic and fish are more likely to key in on it. Like I do for most of my patterns, for the Deceiver I use the adhesive Mylar eyes marketed by Witchcraft. Coating the head with five-minute epoxy serves the dual purpose of protecting the thread wraps and making sure the eyes remain in place.

The Clouser Minnow

Bob Clouser is one of the nicest guys I've ever met. He's as plain as peanut butter and he's created a pattern that fish seem to go for with the same kind of gusto that humans have for the famous sandwich spread. Lefty says that it's the single most effective underwater fly he's ever fished. It's obvious that the word is out because even folks who have just taken up the sport know that this is one pattern they should have in their fly box. Just like the Navy issuing lead-head fishing jigs in their pilots' survival kits, if I were restricted to one fly, the Clouser would be it. Though you would never hear it from him, if anyone had a right to complain about being ripped off, it's Bob Clouser. Everyone I know fishes his pattern. Its in fly shops all over the country, its been written about in fishing magazines, you see it advertised in fly-fishing catalogues. Yet, the little money that Bob makes on the fly, comes primarily from what he sells out of his little shop in Middletown, Pennsylvania. At least he's rich in family and friends. If you ever have the opportunity and want to do some smallmouth fishing on the

Susquehanna, book a trip with him or his son Bobby and you'll be in for one great time. Lefty, who's been privileged to fish just about every place that has water, rates this as his favorite type of fishing.

Aside from the fact that it catches fish, casts like a missile, and doesn't foul, one of the features that I like best about this fly is that it is so easy to tie. Coming from someone with my limited ability, you can take comfort in the fact that you don't have to be blessed with surgeon-like dexterity to tie the Clouser. Like the Deceiver, Bob emphasizes that the Clouser is a style of tying and not so much a specific pattern. The tying process can be modified to tailor the fly to particular locales and species so you can range from tiny streams to the high surf and cast to fish ranging from trout to tuna.

Tying the Clouser Minnow

Hooks: Because so many versions of this fly can be tied, there are a wide variety of hooks that can be used. As a guideline, if you're tying your first Clouser, start with a favorite hook of Bob's, a size 1/0 Mustad 34007.

Eyes: Metal barbell-style eyes are the key to this fly's effectiveness. The eye size will effect the fly's sink rate. For a 1/0 hook, you can use size 1/30 eyes. Before tying them in, I recommend painting them first, red with a black pupil. Attach the tying thread about one-third down the length of the hook shank behind the hook eye. Build a small bump with the thread and place the barbell eyes on the shank immediately behind the small mound of thread. Wrap across the center bar of the eye and under the hook shank using a criss cross wrap from left to right. About 20 tight wraps should hold the eyes firmly in position.

Wing: The wing section can be tied with a variety of materials with bucktail being the most popular. Kinky Fibre and Super Hair are synthetics that are often used instead of bucktail. On smaller versions of the fly, arctic fox and calf tail are ideal for the wing.

To give the fly sparkle, mix in small bunches of varying lengths of Krystal Flash and Flashabou. Although in its original form the Clouser was tied with half the wing material on the bottom section of the hook, standard practice is to tie all the wing material on top of the fly. It should extend back roughly two-and-a-half times the length of the hook. Turn the hook over in the vise so that the point is riding up and the eyes are facing down and attach the material just forward of the eyes. As just about anyone who has fished there will tell you, the top producer for striped bass in the Northeast has been the Clouser tied in a chartreuse-and-white color combination. If you want to duplicate this fly, start by tying in a small portion of white bucktail, follow that with about 12 strands of pearl Krystal Flash, pearl Flashabou or a combination of the two, topped with chartreuse-colored bucktail. My wise friend remarked that she never saw a deer with this color tail and of course she never will. The bucktail has to be dyed and unless you're willing to put up with a big mess, I suggest buying bucktail that has already been colored.

Bob recommends Gloss Head Cement to finish the head. Most of the time I use five-minute epoxy because I find that it does a better job of keeping the barbell eyes in place. I've had the eyes turned out of position from fish crushing it in their jaws as well as from errant casts where I bounced the fly off rocks and pilings. One time while giving a surf-fishing class in Southern California, I smacked a lifeguard truck on the back cast. The lifeguard had never seen anyone using fly rods in the surf and he drove up behind me for a better look. With the sound of the waves, I never heard him approach and since he wasn't accustomed to anyone throwing a line backwards, he was closer to me than he should have been. The bright yellow truck now had a ding in the driver's side door. Fortunately the lifeguard was good natured and acknowledged that he should have been more careful, but I was already thinking of how I could lay the blame on Clouser in the event that I got a bill from Los Angeles County for touch-up work on one of their vehicles. Things might have turned out differently if it was the lifeguard or a passerby that got hit. Regardless of the fly you are using, anytime you're casting in an area where there are people likely to be strolling behind you, it's your responsibility to watch your back casts.

The Cotton Candy

There is no doubt in my mind that the one fly-tier who has influenced me the most is my good friend Bob Popovics from New Jersey. For several years all I knew about Bob's flies was what I had read in the magazines. Some of his silicone-and-epoxy creations were like nothing I had ever seen and Lefty assured me that they fished as well as they looked. I was very anxious to meet the man but with 3,000 miles between us there wasn't much opportunity until we finally caught up with one another at the San Mateo show. We instantly hit it off and became very close friends. If you ever meet him, you'll be instantly drawn to him. He has that kind of personality. And if you ever see him tie (I highly recommend his fly-tying videos) you will witness a true master at the vise. I know a lot of people who would like to lay claim to this, but I rate Bob as the most innovative tier on the saltwater scene today. Unlike some who add a feather or two here, change the color and then designate the fly as a new pattern, Bob's flies represent real breakthroughs both in terms of materials and designs. Similar to my experience with the Deceiver and the Clouser, I've fished his flies in far-ranging places and have always caught fish with them, even on the ones I've tied myself.

I guess of all his patterns, my personal favorite is the Cotton Candy. I first saw it years ago on a trip we made to Martha's Vineyard, the equivalent of the Holy Land for striped bass worshipers. It was around seven in the evening and we were strolling the edge of Lobsterville Beach looking for signs of life. As is often the case in early June, the day before, stripers put on a heart-pumping display as they tore into pods of sand eels, at times not more than ten feet from where we wading in shin-deep water. This time nothing was going on and Bob decides that he wants to see how one of his recently tied Cotton Candy creations looks in the water. I liked it the moment I saw it, but I was thinking billfish in Baja, not bass off the beach. That thought quickly changed on Bob's second cast with the fly that produced a swirl like a powerboat going into gear. "That was one big fish," I yelled to which Bob replied, "Yeah, that's what usually goes after the Candy." In countless trips after that I experienced first hand what he meant. I was the first to

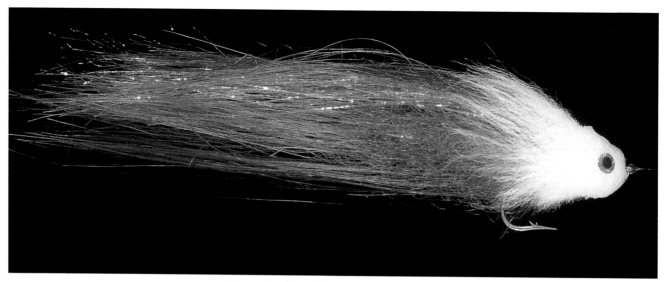

The author's version of a Cotton Candy.

take this fly offshore where I nailed sailfish and striped marlin in Baja. When I was living in Southern California, I successfully fished the Cotton Candy for calico bass, white sea bass, yellowtail and sharks. I've also taken striped bass, and northern pike with it. Bob has a fly specifically designed to imitate squid, (the Shady Lady Squid) but I find the Cotton Candy to be a very effective simulation. I'm convinced that is what the calicos, white sea bass and yellowtail mistake it for when they attempt to eat it.

The key to this fly's construction is the unique combination of materials. The body portion consists of Big Fly Fiber. This material has a dense, crinkled front portion that flows into long, thin-diameter strands. When pulled through the water, it pulsates like it was alive. The head section is composed of stacked bunches of sheep fleece that are trimmed and coated with clear silicone. Trimmed to a blunt, bullet shape, this silicone head enables the fly to push a lot of water on the retrieve. This disturbance coupled with the undulating action of the Big Fly Fiber makes for a very enticing combination. When I fished it on the surface in Saskatchewan, it drove the giant northern pike crazy. More so than any surface popper, the big Candy drew the most violent strikes.

The fly tends to be buoyant, but you can get it down with fast-sinking lines. It will slowly slip into the depths and fish like West Coast calico bass and yellowtail frequently seem to be really turned on by this. Just be prepared to react when the line suddenly stops its downward descent. Speaking of squid flies, most patterns are tied in white. This is fine, however what many anglers do not seem to realize is that squid do change color. So do not hesitate to tie this pattern in various blends of pink, tan and brown. The latter two colors duplicate the so-called "brown bait" (queenfish) on which calicos and occasionally white sea bass feed. Since the Cotton Candy is designed to imitate larger bait, I generally tie mine between 4 and 7 inches long. Some of my billfish Cotton Candies are a foot long. I have had blue sharks go after the big Candies on the off-shore grounds. Once I even had a mako interested, but an overly curious boater ran too close to where I was fishing and the shark swam off.

Tying the Cotton Candy

Hooks: For most inshore applications on species like calico bass, striped bass, white sea bass and yellowtail, one hook I like to use is an Owner Spinnerbait style, model 5320-154 in sizes 2/0 to 5/0. I also tie this pattern with the Mustad 34007, in sizes 3/0 to 5/0.

Body/wing: The body and wing portion of the fly is tied with Big Fly Fiber. This material is easier to work with if you tie in two or three medium size bundles instead of one large bundle. I like to mix in strands of Krystal Flash between and on top of the Big Fly Fiber. As is the case for most of these patterns, I prefer monofilament tying thread because it binds the material very tightly and the clear finish does not obscure any of the colors you may be using for the fly. When placing the fiber on top of the hook shank, take one fairly loose, complete turn of the thread around the bundle before cinching it down tight.

Head/collar: The original pattern is tied with combed out lamb's wool but a less expensive substitute that I find works equally well is a product marketed as Sculpin Wool by Hareline Dubbin, Inc. However, make sure you use only white because the other colors cannot be teased out as easily. A wire brush like the kind sold in pet stores is what you want to use to comb out the fleece. Select a medium size bundle 1 1/2 to 2 inches in length, comb it out flat and lay it on top of the hook shank. Work the material with your fingers so that it partially envelops the shank. As with the Big Fly Fiber, take one complete turn around the material with the thread. Here, the object is to have the fleece flare out and completely envelop the hook shank. Repeat this stacking process right to the hook eye. Trim the head to a fairly blunt, bullet-like shape. Then coat it with a light application of clear silicone. Wearing rubber gloves will prevent your fingers from getting messy. Also a little saliva on your fingertips stroked over the silicone will result in a smooth, slick finish. Just squeeze a small dollop of silicone on your fingertip, place it at the forward portion of the head and smear it toward the rear of the head. Always work the silicone in one direction from front to rear.

Eyes: The peel-off, prismatic eyes from Wicthcraft are what I use for the Cotton Candy. Apply these eyes before the silicone begins to set. Once the eyes are in place, apply a second light coat of silicone to the head and stroke it so it's smooth. Depending on the brand of silicone, several hours drying time may have to elapse before you can fish the fly.

The Jiggy

The Jiggy is an evolution in Bob's Surf Candy series. The Surf Candy has been one of my favorite flies for members of the tuna family like bonito, false albacore and school size yellowfin tuna. It's only shortcoming was the sink rate. The tuna clan does much of its feeding fairly deep in the water column, so one key feature of a fly intended for these species is its rate of descent. How quickly the fly sinks is often the critical factor in determining whether or not you're going to connect with a fish. Bob recognized this and designed the Jiggy as a variation of the Deep Candy which is a weighted version of the original Surf Candy. With the addition of a bead head or "fly head" cone, the Jiggy lives up to its name. With the weight concentrated in the head, the fly will dive nose first and the resulting jigging motion when the fly is retrieved is deadly.

A second important consideration is the fly's profile. Sleek silhouetted baitfish like anchovies are a favorite food source of tuna and the Jiggy offers a very convincing shape. As an added plus, the fly is tied bend-back style so the hook point rides up just like a Clouser Minnow. In blue-water applications with no obstructions this really doesn't mean much, but for inshore locales studded with a variety of hook-snagging structure, the bend-back style is a definite advantage. In Southern California I've taken calicos, halibut and even barred perch on small versions of the fly. Off the beaches in Baja, roosterfish, jack crevalle, and sierra mackerel have all been fooled by it. Stripers in the Northeast have found it to their liking and it's almost impossible to pull it past bluefish without getting bit.

Tying the Jiggy

Hooks: Any of the top-brand saltwater hooks like the Mustad 34007 or Tiemco 911S are ideal for this fly. Depending on the size of the fish, sizes 1 to 3/0 will generally handle most situations. To make sure the bead or cone head will slip over the hook point, you may have to crimp and file down the barb. I usually do this for most of my flies anyway. Taking 3 to 4 wraps around the shank with lead wire and sliding this in to the back of the cone head helps to hold the head in place and provides additional weight to the fly.

Body: Bucktail or a variety of synthetic materials like Kinkyfibre or Polafibre can be used for the body. These are interspersed with several strands of Flashabou or Krystal Flash. Bob prefers bucktail and usually ties the fly with two different color layers. To simulate most baitfish species, you can't go wrong with a white underbelly topped by varying shades of blue or green. For striped bass in the Northeast, white topped with chartreuse is the hot color combination.

Head: Bead head or "fly head" cone.

Eyes: Peel-off, stick-on prismatic eyes. These eyes are affixed to the sides of the Jiggy head. To make sure they remain there, Bob recommends coating them with a bead of five-minute epoxy.

The Whistler Series

Dan Blanton from Northern California originally developed this fly for striped bass in his home waters of San Francisco Bay. The water there tends to be murky, the current is often strong, and as far as stripers are concerned, there is little in the way of surface action. With these considerations in mind, Dan developed the Whistler. He was well aware of the productive potential of lead-head bucktail jigs. Spin and conventional gear anglers who fished them caught more than their share of

Dan Blanton's lightly modified Whistler.

striped bass and Dan wanted a fly to incorporate the jig's features. The Whistler does so admirably. The first time I used one was in the jungle rivers of Costa Rica. Dan was the first to use his fly on deep-water tarpon down there and it proved to be the hot ticket. It is still one of my favorite patterns for Costa Rican tarpon. But even when it comes to U.S coastal waters, I never venture forth without a few Whistlers in my box. When I need to get a fly down, when a large silhouette is desirable, and when I want an up-and-down jigging motion on the retrieve, I turn to the Whistler. I've taken many bonito on smaller, sparsely tied versions, but this fly really comes into its own tied full-bodied.

Like the Deep Candy and Clouser, the Whistler derives its diving characteristics from the fact that the weight is concentrated in the head portion of the fly. Dan originally tied the fly with bead-chain eyes. He named it after the sound it made going through the air. However, you increase the fly's sink rate by substituting lead dumbbell eyes. This can be augmented by wrapping the hook shank with lead wire.

Tying the Whistler

Hooks: Dan prefers a fairly short-shank hook, such as a Mustad 9175 or an Eagle Claw 254SS. For many coastal species like calicos, sand bass, white sea bass, stripers and yellowtail, a size 3/0 or 4/0 hook works fine.

Eyes: Tie in a pair of bead-chain or lead dumbbell eyes behind the hook eye. If you want you to add lead wire wraps, do so after tying in the eyes.

Tail: The tail is tied at the rear of the hook and in its original configuration, it consisted of three separate bundles of bucktail stacked to form a high vertical wing. Taper the stubs as you tie in each bundle to form a neat sloping foundation. In the early Whistler series, Dan formed a thin red stripe along each side of the wing by tying in approximately ten strands of red bucktail on either side. If you like, you can use a few strands of red Flashabou for the bucktail and tie these in along each side of the fly. The fly's attractor potential can be enhanced considerably by mixing in some of this flash material in the tail section and adding pairs of saddle hackles.

Collar: Using a length of medium-size red chenille, take two turns around the hook shank and tie it off. Then take three, long webby saddle hackles and tie them individually in front of the chenille collar. Palmer wrap each of the hackles forward filling in the gap between the collar and the eyes. Sometimes I use sheep fleece for the collar instead of the palmered hackle.

Like the other patterns, the Whistler can be tied in a variety of colors. Especially for stripers in the Northeast, I've had the best results with a white tail and red collar. I also like to add two grizzly neck hackles on either side.

The Crease Fly

I met Captain Joe Blados years ago on what was then one of my annual summer excursions back to the Northeast. I was giving a seminar to the Salty Fly Rodders of New York and Joe invited me to go fishing with him. A good piece of advice: never refuse an invitation from an experienced local angler. We were in his home waters on the north shore of eastern Long Island and the striped bass were in an obliging mood. That's when I first saw his Crease Fly in action. After he hooked three nice bass in a half-hour's time, I knew it was time to change flies. Joe was fishing his Crease Fly on a floating line and in the dim light of dawn, I could see the little wake it left as it worked its way across the surface like a crippled baitfish. The stripers couldn't seem to leave it alone. Joe actually hooked and landed three bass, but he was also experiencing a good number of violent surface strikes. We didn't see all of them, but we certainly heard them.

of someone who knows what they're doing, this method can be particularly effective on barracuda and for awhile, he was getting a strike on almost every cast. Though I didn't keep pace, we were both surprised at how often this fly was getting bit. The main disadvantage I faced was the fly's relatively slow sink rate. It took me longer to reach the barracuda's feeding zone. According to the depth finder, they were concentrated about 25 feet down. My friend was using a jig that was designated as "surface iron," but it only took a few seconds for the lure to get to the desired depth. I had to wait longer for the lead-core line to sink, and as it did so, a bow developed in the line because of the buoyant fly. However, as line was stripped in, the fly dove deeper and this is when the barracuda would strike it.

Over the last few years, the Crease Fly has accounted for good numbers of barracuda, calico bass and kelp paddy yellowtail, but the most fun has been with surface-feeding yellowfin tuna. I still fish the fly with a fast-sinking line, but when tuna are crashing the surface,

Captain Joe Blados's Crease Fly.

Already I was thinking of other locales and species and I asked him how the fly worked on a fast-sinking line. He assured me that it was equally as deadly. I returned to Southern California a few weeks later where I first put it to the test in a barracuda bite that had developed a little north of Marina Del Rey. My friend who owned the skiff was a confirmed conventional tackle fisherman who loved to throw the "iron," (the local designation for elongated metal jigs). In the hands

I begin retrieving the fly as soon as it lands on the water. This way, the naturally buoyant fly will remain right on the surface driving the tuna crazy with its erratic, zigzag swimming motion. The best way to achieve this action is by means of a two-handed retrieve.

Tying the Crease Fly

Hooks: To achieve the desired body profile, a long-shank hook like the Mustad 34011 is needed. Another good choice is the Eagle Claw 66SS. This is an offset hook that can easily be straightened with pliers. It is also slightly heavier than a 34011 and for that reason I use it for those applications where I want the fly to get down as quickly as possible.

Tail: To simulate an anchovy or similar baitfish, tie in a bundle of white bucktail. You can also use synthetic materials like Kinkyfibre or Polarfibre. For the topping, use the same material you started with only in a darker shade. Grey, green and blue shades all make for effective baitfish simulations. If you cannot find these colors, use white material and color it the desired shade with water-proof marking pens. A few strands of peacock herl or Krystal Flash can also be added. Begin tying the tail by placing the material on top of the hook shank about 1/4 inch behind the hook eye. Cut the material on a bias so it forms a taper at the point where it is tied to the shank. Make sure to cover the entire top portion of the shank with the tail material. This will serve as a foundation for the foam body.

Body: The body material is what distinguishes the Crease Fly from most other patterns. The material is available in sheet form from craft stores and is marketed under different labels such as Live Body Foam, Fun Foam, and Imagi-Foam. Buy the white-colored foam. Hold the foam against the hook and mark off a section that approximates the length of the hook shank, measuring from a point immediately behind the hook eye. The rear of the body should extend about a 1/4 inch past the hook point. Fold the foam over the hook shank. At its widest point, the body should be between 1/2 to 3/4 of an inch. When you have a body silhouette that conforms to the hook size, cut the folded bottom portion of the foam where it will be glued to the hook shank. Taper the top rear section so that it neatly encases a front portion of the tail. Place the body over the hook so that the shank is at the very bottom of the folded foam halves. You don't want to bury the hook shank deep inside the fold. This will destroy the action of the fly. Make sure the hook is straight and then apply a gel-type CA glue (like Zap-A-Gap) to the underside of the body where it encases the hook shank. The body is now complete except for the color scheme and this is easily accomplished by means of water-proof permanent marking pens. For baitfish imitations, leave the bottom half of the sides and underbelly white. The top half sections can be colored various shades of green or blue. A nice effect can be achieved by wiping the markings with tissue paper. This blends the color into the foam. You can also apply Mylar sheeting and then color it.

Eyes: Use the stick-on prismatic eyes from Witchcraft. To make sure these remain affixed, apply a light coat of 5-minute epoxy. A light epoxy coat applied to the color markings on the sides of the foam body makes for an attractive shiny finish.

The Tres Generation Fly

This fly was developed by Dale Hightower. Dale is a native Southern Californian who has been fishing the area practically since he could walk. His father and three brothers all work in the tackle industry so I guess you could say he grew up in a fishing family. Dale's love for the sport blossomed at an early age and when it came time for him to choose a career, he followed his father and brothers and made fishing his livelihood.

Similar to my own background, Dale started fishing primarily with conventional and spinning gear. He also logged a good deal of time on Southland party boats which is a great way to thoroughly familiarize yourself with the area's saltwater fishery. One of the lessons he learned was that where artificial lures were concerned, chrome jigs and trolling feathers outfished almost everything else. When he started fly-fishing, Dale searched for patterns that incorporated the particular qualities of each of these lures, but he wasn't satisfied with what he found. This gave him the impetus to develop something on his own.

His first efforts were aimed at trying to simulate the properties of chrome metal jigs. He fashioned a head from masking tape, wrapping it behind the hook eye until he had a diameter approximately the size of a laundry marking pen. For the body, he used pre-cut sheets of Witchcraft prismatic strips and taped them around the masking tape head. A pair of doll eyes were glued to the head and coated with 5-minute epoxy. The fly had good reflective qualities, but its swimming action was poor. Disappointed, he set aside the fly and almost forgot about it. Almost two years later, he was rummaging through his fly-tying materials and found a length of pearlescent tubing. This material suddenly triggered thoughts about his earlier efforts and Dale immediately decided that the tubing would make an ideal body for his fly. He slid the tubing over the masking tape head, trimmed it to approximate the size of baitfish like anchovies and smelt and fished the creation in Baja. To his delight, the fly worked great. It had all the reflective qualities of chrome jigs and exhibited an enticing darting motion in the water.

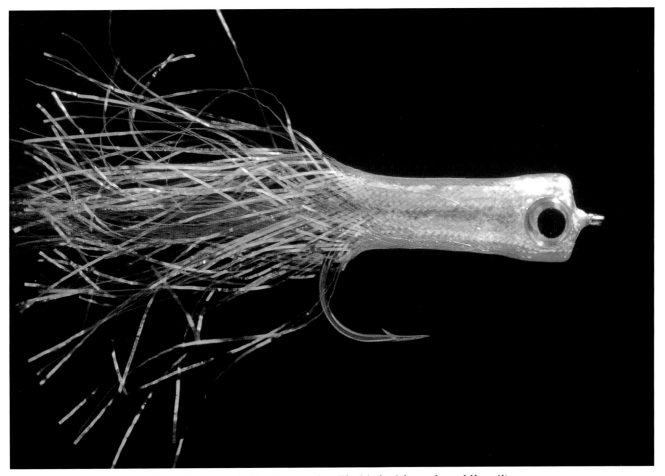

Dale Hightower's Tres Generation Fly (tied without the saddle tail).

Despite its success, Dale wanted to take the fly one step further. Stage three (hence the name, tres generations) involved the addition of a tail section in the form of saddle hackles. The fly now embodies the appeal of metal jigs coupled with the attractive qualities of undulating feathers. In addition, it is translucent, and barracuda, bonito, calico bass, jack crevalle, yellowtail, roosterfish have all displayed an eagerness to try and eat it.

Tying the Tres Generation Fly

Hooks: Dale prefers the Owner Spinnerbait style (5320) in sizes 1/0 to 5/0.

Head: When using 1/0 to 3/0 size hooks, build a 1/4-inch-diameter head by wrapping 1/2-inch-wide stripping or masking tape around the hook shank 1/8 inch behind the hook eye. With 4/0 and 5/0 hooks, build a 1/2-inch diameter head.

Tail: On the smaller version of this fly with 1/0 and 3/0 hooks, use 4 to 6 saddle hackles splayed out tarpon style. For most conditions, I recommend white hackles as probably the best choice. Tie them in on top of the hook shank at the bend of the hook. Cut the thread. On larger flies where you may want a fuller profile, use wider neck hackles. For added flash, tie in a few strands of Krystal Flash or Flashabou alongside the hackle.

Body: Depending on the size of the fly desired, use either medium or large pearlescent Flashabou Minnow Body Tubing. Fray one end to equal the length of the tail feathers and push the tubing over the taped head to a point where the frayed ends are even with the tail feathers. Retie the thread immediately behind the hook eye. Grasp the front end of the tubing and take two loose turns of thread around the tubing. Then pull the thread tight and take several more turns to secure the tubing to the hook shank. Trim off any strands that have frayed and wrap over the remaining butts to form a smooth, tapered head. At this stage any color patterns can easily be created with marking pens. Stick on a pair of prismatic eyes. Use 5/16-inch eyes for large flies and 1/4 inch for smaller versions. Coat the eyes and body with five-minute epoxy.

CHAPTER 5

Casting Your Line Upon The Waters

Casting and Presentation Strategies

Make no mistake about it. Fly-fishing involves fly-casting and to attain any degree of proficiency as a fly-fisher, particularly in the saltwater realm, you not only must know how to cast, you must know how to cast well. This is a topic unto itself and I am making the assumption that most of those interested in a book of this type will have already managed some degree of mastery with the long rod. If you want to learn more about this fascinating game or simply hone your technique, two excellent sources I can recommend are Ed Jaworoski's book appropriately entitled, *The Cast*, and a video by the master himself, entitled "Casting with Lefty Kreh."

The inability to get the fly to the fish is not only a frustrating experience for the angler, it can also be maddening for others you are with, like the guide or a fellow angler. Most fly-fishing guides will tell you that the major source of difficulty they experience with clients lies in the angler's lack of casting technique. And the harder the guide has to work to get the angler into position, the more frustrating the experience becomes when the angler cannot make the delivery. Some of the most dramatic and saddening instances of faulty casting occur in sight-fishing on shallow-water flats.

Without a doubt this is my favorite fly-fishing scenario. Aside from the other sensory inputs, sight-fishing the shallows is the premier visual experience. Even when you're not the one on the casting platform, the fact that you can see the quarry makes it an exciting time for all. Whether you're in the tropics angling for bonefish or permit or on a flat in the Northeast hunting striped bass, skinny-water sight-fishing is probably the most challenging dimension fly-fishing has to offer. It's unfortunate though that so many anglers come up short simply because they cannot meet the

Tom Dorsey casts a line along a mangrove channel.

casting requirements. Delivery is everything and if your casting is not proficient, the contest shifts in the fish's favor the moment you begin to move the rod.

Fishing in the Yucatan some years back from Casa Blanca lodge, my partner for the week was an experienced trout fisherman from Colorado. His casting may have been adequate for inland streams but he found himself way out of his league on these pristine flats off Mexico's East Coast. There was no equipment problem here, because I outfitted him with my own top-quality gear; a Thomas and Thomas Horizon 9-foot, 10-weight rod, an Islander large arbor 4.0 reel and a brand-new Scientific Anglers Mastery weight-forward line. Poling us into position at the edge of a meandering channel that snaked across the flat, our small-framed Mayan guide worked up a sweat that saturated him like a cluster of burst water balloons. But it was well worth the effort as we could plainly see the dorsal fins of three permit swaying above the surface like giant blades of grass. Having thrown many softballs in my youth, I guessed that the fish were about 60 feet off our bow. The guide asked, *Listo?* ("are you ready?") and my friend begins to flail the rod like he was trying to ward off a hive of killer bees. I couldn't count how many false casts but there had to be at least a half dozen, all of them with little effect as the line seemed to lengthen at about the same rate as sap dribbling from a tree. Couple that with the parade of wavelets shooting out from the boat as my partner rocked back and forth trying to coax more line out, and it's a wonder that the permit lingered as long as they did before gliding into the comfort zone of the deeper channel. The guide looks at me and mutters, *"Que lastima,"* which roughly translates, "what a shame." I didn't know whether he was referring to himself and the hundreds of yards of poling against the current he just endured or my hapless friend who blew an excellent chance for his first permit. I was also very frustrated. I wanted to see my friend hook this fish, however when it soon became apparent that he could not execute the cast, I was wishing that it was me who was on the platform. Protocol dictates that you bear with the situation until it's your turn to cast but it doesn't make it any easier to stand by and witness such a wasted opportunity.

It was obvious this fellow did not even have the basics down and in this type of flats fishing, it takes more than a mastery of mere fundamentals to be consistently successful. Just consider what you are up against. The water is shallow and is clear as a contact lens. And despite the fact that species like bonefish and permit frequent such habitat as familiar feeding zones, the fact that they can be so easily identified by a variety of potential predators, makes them extremely wary. Even those at the top of the predator hierarchy can be skittish in the shallows. In the Florida Keys in the early seventies I had my first fly-rod shark encounters casting to lemon and blacktip sharks in knee-deep water with little fear of being attacked. All I had to do was smack the water with my hand and these chainsaws with fins would streak across the flat like fighters screaming off the flight deck. But given just a few feet more water depth, there is no way I would relish being in the water with them, especially when they are searching for a meal.

So in addition to casting fundamentals, one of the requirements for this type of fishing is finesse casting. First of all, as in all aspects of this sport, you should strive for a minimum of false casts. False casting is essentially down time. The fish are in the water, not in the air and on the flats there are two additional considerations. Fish tend to move more erratically in the shallows. If it takes a number of false casts to work out a sufficient length of line, by the time the final forward cast is made, the fish may be moving in a different direction. Furthermore, fish can be easily spooked by a line passing overhead, so the more false casts you make, the greater the odds of alarming fish, some of which you may not have even seen. A second component of finesse casting is accuracy. Even if you can throw a long length of line with a minimum of false casts, on the flats at least, if you cannot place the fly in the target zone, more often than not you will come up empty handed.

I learned that the hard way in some of my early excursions to the Keys and the Marquesas in the seventies. On one such outing Lefty Kreh, who was living in Miami at the time, was gracious enough to loan myself and two friends, Lou Tabory and Pete Kriewald, his 16-foot Hewes Bonefisher skiff. Lefty was instrumental in the design of this now classic flats skiff and I was thrilled to get a chance to fish the Marquesas, which at the time, was still relatively untouched, at least by fly-fishers. Lefty even marked off some of his favorite spots on the chart. Well, we got into fish all right, but the "catchin" as they say, wasn't so easy.

All of us were proficient with the fly rod in terms of casting distance, but up to this time our fly-fishing experience had primarily been confined to tossing flies at blitzing schools of bluefish and stripers. Acres of surface-breaking fish are an easy target. Ideally you want to place the fly at the edge of a feeding school to avoid alarming the others. However, the likelihood of scaring off ravenous blues and bass with fly-rod poppers and streamers is pretty slim, so even if your casts do not quite land where you intend, there isn't much harm done. The same is true when casting to likely holding spots like rocks, rip lines and drop-offs. The targets are usually large and they are stationary. Consequently, pinpoint accuracy was something we did not really have to worry about.

The situation is similar to what I experienced on the long-range trips out of San Diego where occasionally I logged deckhand duty as a tradeoff for fishing time. Aside from helping passengers catch fish, a major concern on these trips is safety. When you have 18 to 30 passengers, half of whom may be simultaneously casting baits or metal lures, you have to constantly remind everyone to be careful not to hook their fellow passengers. The accuracy issue here was making sure no one was hit with a hook. To help prevent this, everyone was instructed to turn their heads to the rear and watch their bait or lure as they made their cast. The familiar saying went something to the effect that, "the ocean is a big target, you'll be sure to hit it, we don't need a hook in the person standing next to you." In situations where you are fishing wide-open expanses of water, blind casting where there is no specific target is the standard practice and accuracy seldom plays a major role. That is usually not the case however, on the flats.

Reflecting back on that early Marquesas trip, I realize that our lack of concern in this area was all too apparent. We blew fish after fish with misplaced casts. I want to emphasize that distance was seldom the problem. As novices on the flats, our handicap was primarily a lack of accuracy in our casts. My first opportunity for a permit was a complete disaster because of a misplaced cast. In partial defense, you have to bear in mind that at the time, only a handful of these extremely wary members of the jack family had ever been taken on fly. Lefty had one mounted on his office wall that was about half the size of a dinner plate. When I naively remarked that it must have been a baby, he exploded into a tirade of how difficult these fish were to take on fly gear. Given their almost mystical reputation as the stellar species of the flats, my panic button was the first to go off when we spotted a manhole-size specimen about 75 feet to the port side of the skiff. To say that my emotional circuits were on overload would be an understatement. Lou was poling the skiff and he didn't want to approach any further for fear of spooking the fish. He asked if I thought I could make the cast, and naturally I said yes. I sure as heck did not want to relinquish my turn on the

casting platform. At the time, because I was relatively new to the fly-fishing game, my major concern was distance. Of course, I should have also been concentrating on where to place the fly. Lefty had drilled us on the importance of getting the fly in front of the fish. It's easy to understand that in the Darwin-scripted, eat-or-be-eaten world these creatures inhabit, prey does not approach the predator from behind. You can scare the hell out of a hundred-pound tarpon merely by dropping a 3-inch fly behind its tail fin. In nature's scheme of things it just does not happen that way.

That is basically what I did when I cast to the permit. I was using a Scientific Anglers 9-foot 8-weight fly rod because bonefish were our main quarry. That fiberglass stick seems woefully slow by today's standards but back then it was considered state-of-the-art. I didn't know enough about permit to be using a weighted crab fly and a heavier 10-weight rod to facilitate its delivery. Permit were sort of an afterthought. I felt I would be lucky just to see one. The fly I had on was an overgrown version of a standard bonefish pattern. The question of whether a permit would have ever been attracted to it is a moot one because my cast put the fly practically on its dorsal fin. The resulting effect was like throwing the anchor overboard. At least we all had a good laugh and the permit got its exercise for the day. By the way, just to keep the record straight, Lou and Pete both muffed their share of fish with poorly placed casts. Lou spooked a log-sized barracuda that looked almost half the length of the push poll and Pete coaxed three tarpon off the flat with a long cast that unfortunately landed opposite of where nature intended them to take food.

Not only do your casts have to be accurate, in many cases they also have to be fast. Quick casts are most often referred to in the context of flats fishing but they are equally important any time fish are on the move. Fish on the feed are a good example. Like pigeons following free handouts in the park, game fish make tracks to where the food is. Bluefish, striped bass, and members of the tuna family like bonito, false albacore, bluefin, yellowfin and skipjack are famous for ambushing pods of terrified baitfish, decimating their ranks and then hightailing it elsewhere in search of fresh prey. Under circumstances like these, the ability to fire out quick, accurate casts often spells the difference between a solid hookup and a fishless retrieve.

The speed that I am referring to is in the delivery, not the casting stroke. The distinction is easy to make on paper, out on the water it can be a different ball game. I guess it amounts to the fishing version of buck fever. In the latter instance the prospective hunter does very well on the shooting range but when the moment of truth arrives and the quarry is in the cross hairs, things seem to fall apart.

Last year, staked out on a flat in northeast Florida with my friend Corbett Davis, Jr. and guide Steve Kilpatrick, we witnessed a classic example of this phenomenon. We were the second boat to arrive so our chances of intercepting tarpon that had not yet been alerted by the first boat were somewhat compromised. When there were no fish cruising by, the fellow in the other boat passed the time by making practice casts. Corbett, who is a very accomplished fly-fisher in his own right, remarked at how proficient he was. But every time a tarpon approached, things changed dramatically. He manipulated the rod like a baton in the hands of a mad conductor and the previously tight loops grew wide enough to accommodate the family car. It was obvious that he could not maintain good casting form precisely when it was needed most. In his hurried efforts to deliver the fly on time, the casts either fell woefully short of the target, or arrived so late that the tarpon was now in our casting range.

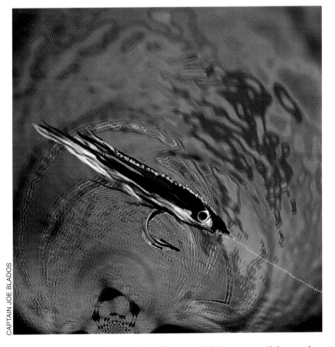

CAPTAIN JOE BLADOS

In trying to deliver the fly as quickly as possible to the fish, proper casting form remains unchanged. Instead, the speed in delivery is a function of advance preparation. Prior to any initial cast, the fly line should be stretched to remove any coils that may have formed as a result of the line being wound on the spool. I have to admit that this is something I often fail to do and too many times I

pay for it with a muffed cast because the line will tangle before it ever clears the second stripping guide. In my haste to cast to a big striper off the east end of Long Island a couple seasons back, the fly never got near the fish because the fly line was hopelessly tangled. I should have known better, but everything was delayed that day from getting stuck in traffic, to the ferry ride over to Orient Point. I finally met up with my good friend and guide Joe Blados, who wasted little time in poling me to one of the biggest stripers I've ever seen on the eastern Long Island flats. I had just finished rigging my 9-weight outfit and did not want to take the extra time to stretch the line. It was lying at my feet in coils that resembled the Slinky spring I used to play with as a kid. Joe just laughed and mumbled something about practicing what you preach.

The second order of business is to make sure that the heavier, belly section of the fly line lies on top of the pile of line that has been pulled from the reel in preparation for the cast. The fly line is in proper order when it is wound on the reel's spool. However, when it is initially stripped from the reel, the heavier tapered section is the first to fall into a pile followed by the thinner-diameter running line. What this means is that the first cast attempted will very likely result in a messy tangle because the thick belly section which must pass through the rod-tip first has to climb out from under the remaining running line. To make sure this doesn't happen when you're casting to a fish, make a preliminary cast to rearrange the fly line in the proper order. I like to refer to this as a sacrificial cast because essentially that's what it is. If the line is likely to foul, you want it to happen on a cast that is inconsequential, not when you've spotted a fish you would like to jump on your fly.

It is surprising how many times even experienced fly-fishers fail to take these important preliminary steps. Another instance of my own lack of attention in this respect took place on an early San Diego long-range trip and cost me my first opportunity to take an albacore on fly. The albies, as they're sometimes referred to in the Southern California party boat circuit, were down off Baja, approximately 320 miles south of the border. Not to be confused with the false albacore that have become favorite targets of East Coast fly-fishers, these tuna are the genuine, long-finned specimens that get top billing as white-meat tuna. These jet-set members of the tuna clan are noted not only for their long migration patterns, they are also widely recognized as a "here today, gone tomorrow" type of species because of their penchant for suddenly vacating an area in search of more abundant food sources. Realizing this, I knew that a four-day trip on one of the long-range boats operating out of Fisherman's Landing in San Diego would give me my best shot at the elusive longfin. I booked a spot on the flagship of the fleet, *The Royal Polaris.* I had taken my first yellowfin on fly from her decks years before on a 16-day trip and was confident that I could follow suit with an albacore. The major obstacle I would face is the same problem I confronted on previous trips. I would be the sole angler using fly gear. This was long before the advent of long-range trips specially tailored for fly-fishers so it was necessary to learn to work your way around the 25 or so other anglers tossing live bait and metal lures. Needless to say, I sacrificed considerable fishing time because the opportunity to slip into one of the stern corners to make a cast was very limited and the bow

Following standard procedure, after an albacore had been hooked and promptly wrenched in on one of the stout trolling lines, the deckhand began chumming with live anchovies as the boat continued to slide forward after the engines were put in neutral. With all the chum in the water this can be a prime time to toss an offering, but to avoid tangles, the drill is that no one is to cast until the deckhand yells that it is okay to do so. I stripped out about 45 feet of line with the first 12 feet outside the rod tip. When the deckhand gave the signal, I roll cast the section of line outside the rod tip, made a back cast and then experienced an abrupt stop on the forward cast. The remaining line on deck shot up to the first stripping guide in a tangled mess that looked like a wad of linguini. I was yelling expletives that would never pass editorial muster, but the simple fact is that I was at

The master, Lefty Kreh, giving an impromptu casting lesson.

section was always occupied. On the plus side, from all my years of riding these boats I knew all the deckhands on this trip, and the owner/skipper, Frank LoPreste is a good friend. The fact that I was the first angler to ever use fly gear on one of these trips years before lent a small measure of credibility to what I was trying to do, but fly-fishing was still a novelty for the passengers and crew. Fortunately, everyone on board was anxious to see me tie into a longfin with this "trout gear," and on the afternoon of our third day out, I was given my chance. By this time most passengers had caught enough albacore to make tuna salad for the next decade, and I was finally allowed to take a position in the port corner.

fault for not taking the time to rearrange the fly line beforehand. Evidently, this was not a large school of fish. Only a couple of albies were taken on bait and by the time I had things squared away, it was time to move on and search for new action. Unfortunately, as far as the albacore were concerned, no more were taken on that trip and we spent the last day without a single trolling stop.

Aside from making that first preliminary cast to arrange the fly line in the proper order, a second lesson learned on that outing was to always have a backup outfit rigged and ready to go. In fly-fishing, a certain measure of line tangles is inevitable even when you do everything right. If the action is hot, you do not want to waste valuable time trying to straighten out a snarled mess. To maximize your opportunities, simply grab another outfit and have a go at it. Obviously this isn't always practical, but whenever feasible, multiple outfits are good insurance that you will not come up short when the bite is on. It bears emphasizing that the additional outfit should be ready to pick up and cast. Rods that are still in their tubes, and reels tucked in their cases are of little use when fish are actively feeding and you have to make a cast now.

Now that I look back on it, it seems pretty funny, but at the time I didn't think so. My friend John Napoli whom I referred to in Chapter One, besides being a recognized tournament caster is also a lawyer so I have to be careful about what I say. We were in my former home waters, fishing bonito in Redondo's King Harbor. Up until the mid-1980s, King Harbor boasted some of the world's best bonito fishing. Regardless of the tide, the weather, or the season, it was not uncommon to take 10 to 15 bonito in the five-pound class in only a couple of hours of fishing. My house was only five minutes from the harbor and for years I averaged 300 days a year tossing flies at the "boneheads." John's fishing experience was confined primarily to dry-fly excursions for wary trout, but he was eager to sample this fishery I kept raving about that was so close to home.

Most of my fishing in the harbor took place from atop the breakwater. It was an ideal situation for a fly-rodder because you cast into the harbor and the wind was almost always at your back. John however, likes to keep what he refers to as "unnecessary physical exertion" to a minimum, so rock hopping the breakwater was out of the question. We rented a skiff, and anchored about 100 feet from the live-bait receiver. It was literally only a matter of minutes before we were surrounded by bonito busting bait that were being generously tossed in our direction by a friend who was working on the receiver.

As an aside, when I moved to Southern California with my family when I was a freshman in high school, my first summer job was on the bait receiver in the harbor. My primary task consisted of dispensing live bait (mostly in the form of anchovies) to the commercial passenger-carrying sport boats that operated out of Redondo. To this day it still ranks as the best job I ever had. I was in fishermen's heaven. The trouble is, like most good things it didn't last. I spent countless hours hooked up to bonito I chummed to within feet of the receiver. Finally, one day when there wasn't enough bait for the sport boats because I had used most of it for chum, I got the ax.

It's about 30 years later, and I'm still addicted to the glorious sensations these dynamos of the tuna family provide at the end of a line, only now I'm doing it with fly gear. The bonito are going crazy ripping into tightly concentrated schools of bait (on the West Coast these are referred to as "meatballs") and playing true to the code of the gentleman, I give John the opportunity to cast first. He graciously accepted, picked up his rod and launched into a sequence that I couldn't believe I was witnessing. John became totally enamored with his casts. He's making cast after cast, the bonito are practically eating the paint off the boat and I cannot make a presentation until his lust for perfect loops is satiated. We all know that lawyers sometimes have a hard time listening, so I informed him in as direct a fashion as possible, that if he could manage to let his fly actually make contact with the water, he might have a chance to enjoy another facet of the sport. In fairness, John can make speedy, accurate casts with the best of them. In fact, when my casting needs a little fine-tuning, I go to John. He knows the importance of quick presentations, but his love for casting is such that it sometimes takes precedence over hooking fish.

In the saltwater fly-fishing schools I would conduct for Marriott's Fly-fishing Store in Fullerton, California, King Harbor was the site we would use to get students out on the water. One fellow who took the class was a trout guide from Oregon. I will not mention his name because in the ten years that I taught these weekend classes, he was only the second person to hook himself with a fly. I was showing him how to execute a speed cast. This is an advanced technique normally not covered in an introductory class but this young man knew how to handle a fly rod and was anxious to expand his repertoire of casting skills.

After line has been stripped from the reel and arranged in proper order for the cast, about 12 to 15 feet of the fly line remains outside the rod tip. The exact length is a function of the taper of the fly line you are using. With lines that have a fairly short, blunt taper (sometimes marketed as saltwater tapers), you don't need as much hanging from the tip as you do with lines that have a more gradual taper. The second step involves grasping the fly between the thumb and first finger of your line hand. This is where the guide made his mistake. I did not realize that the hook point was resting against his thumb. As soon as a fish is spotted, the object is to make a quick, sharp back cast which will pluck the fly from your fingers. Unfortunately, that did not happen. Instead, the force of the line flying behind on the back cast drove the hook into his thumb. I always made sure all the students mashed the barbs down on their flies, so pulling it out was not a problem. He took a second go at it and managed to get it right. The slight resistance of the fly being plucked from your fingers helps load the rod on the initial back cast. This sets you up for the following forward cast, which in many cases is all that you'll need to get the fly to the fish. If more distance is required, extend some line on the first forward cast, make a second back cast followed by the second and final forward cast. You can also extend line on the back cast. I was demonstrating this technique to a Finnish angler one season on the Kenai River in Alaska. While trying to extend line on the back cast, the line slipped through his fingers and landed in a riffle behind him. As he went to lift the fly from the water to try it again, he found himself hooked to a nice king salmon. There was a language barrier and to this day I'm sure he's convinced that this is some odd style of American casting.

Two additional concerns that also play a part in the presentation strategy are the manner in which the line is lifted off the water in preparation for the cast, and how it lands on the water after the cast. Too many fly-fishers pay only scant attention to these matters, but they can be just as important as the speed and accuracy of the delivery. I witnessed a graphic example of this when fishing with Joe Blados on the Long Island flats a few years ago.

The big three of the tropical flats—bonefish, tarpon and permit—garner most of the press when it comes to accounts of ultra-wary fish on windowpane-clear flats. True enough. However, it's a mistake to think that sight-fishing stripers in the shallows is any less demanding. In years of pursuing all four species, I can attest that bass on the flats can be every bit as skittish as their more exotic, southern-based cousins. Apparently though, the fellow who chartered Joe for the day that I was invited along to take pictures, did not realize how important it was to exercise proper line control before and after the cast. This New York City angler cast a line with a degree of skill you normally would not expect from someone who spends practically all of their time in the confines of a major metropolis. He learned his craft well. However, after a few fruitless casts to cruising stripers, it was evident that most of his casting practice did not take place on the water. When he lifted the weight-forward floating line from the water to make the back cast, the commotion on the surface was like Moses parting the Red Sea. Time after time, we saw bass high speed it from

the area before the fly ever hit the water on the forward cast. We were so intensely focused on the fish, that it took several frustrating encounters before Joe realized that the stripers were being spooked by the surface disturbance created as the line was ripped from the water. Since this fellow was an accomplished caster, he easily made the necessary adjustment. Instead of bending his elbow to lift the line off the water, I told him to simultaniously lift and pull back with his arm. This gets the line moving and enables you to lift it from the water with minimum surface disturbance. The fly line glides smoothly from the surface almost like a leaf being blown from the water. Lifting the line in this manner, loads the rod with maximum efficiency because the rod must overcome the resistance of the line floating on the surface. This sets the stage for a well-executed back cast and forward cast.

A few days later, about eight miles north of where Joe had taken us, I had the privilege of watching Lefty Kreh practice what he teaches as he cast to a striper that was cruising the edge of an eelgrass bed along a shallow flat. I'm fortunate to spend quite a bit of time with Lefty at the various fishing shows we work together, and I take advantage of every opportunity to watch him perform at the casting pools. But with our busy schedules, it's not all that often we have the opportunity to make trips together. If you want to sharpen your angling skills, any time spent with Lefty is precious time, but there's an extra-special dimension when you can see him in action on the water. It's sort of like watching a golf pro take putting practice on artificial turf, compared to seeing one perform on a real green with the contour of a potato chip. In either case, you won't be disappointed. When you have the right stuff, it manifests itself in staged sessions as well as in the playing field. There are a number of casters who look very good in the confines of a sterile, wind-free auditorium, but fall apart when they're out on the water confronting Mother Nature in the raw. Having been close friends with Lefty for almost forty years, I can assure you that he doesn't fall into that category. And watching him deliver the fly to that striper confirmed that he can still "walk the walk" even at seventy-plus years.

He had just made a cast to a bass that refused a beautifully tied fly he helped popularize for Bob Clouser. For much of the striper season in the Northeast, a three- to four-inch, chartreuse-and-white Clouser Minnow is the hot ticket. I guess if I were limited to one fly for stripers, this would be it. Bear in mind however, that in all realms of this sport, and particularly in fly-fishing, there is never a sure thing and you will get humbled. You can have a great fly coupled with a textbook-perfect presentation and still get refusals. Lefty knows this as well as anyone but it still didn't stop him from making some derogatory remarks about that fussy bass.

His guide that day was Paul Dixon, a transplanted Californian who is one of the pioneers of Northeast flats fishing. Just as Lefty was describing how dumb the bass was for failing to eat his fly, Paul pointed to the striper that was swimming alongside the eel grass. In a mirror image of the photo sequences in one of his books, *Casting with Lefty Kreh*, Lefty lifted the line from the water with the delicacy of a cat treading on cotton balls. He executed an arrow-straight back cast, followed by a forward cast with a loop so tight that it could probably fit in the keyhole of a door lock. Lefty directed the cast so the fly would come to a stop in the air before it landed on the water. Now all he had to do was lower the rod. This caused the fly to land on the water as unobtrusively as a feather being blown by the wind. Manipulating the fly line in this manner on both the back cast and forward cast are key to a stealth-like presentation to wary fish on clear, shallow-water flats. By contrast, tearing line off the water with the commotion of a jet ski or having the line land on the water like a fat man doing a belly dive, is akin

the authority of a Marine Corps DI. Lefty is not adverse to taking orders, but he was quick to remind Paul that he wanted to give the fly a chance to sink a few feet to where the bass could attack it head on. The Clouser was weighted with 1/2-ounce lead dumbbell eyes, but with a floating line and moderate current, you cannot begin to immediately strip line as soon as the fly lands on the water, otherwise it will ride too close to the surface. The fish will either fail to see the fly, or be frightened off if it looks up and sees the boat. Lefty had calculated all this before he even made the cast, and despite Paul's urgent prompting, he knew when to begin stripping line. Seconds later when the rod arched toward the water like it was being drawn by a giant magnet, it was obvious that Lefty's timing was perfect. The striper grabbed the fly, felt the hook, realized it made a mistake, and put everything into high gear trying to rid itself of this foreign object. I'm guessing that it was the first time the bass ever encountered a situation like this. For Lefty, on the other hand, it was a scene that he played out thousands of times before on countless varieties of fish. From the standpoint of experience alone, the odds were in Mr. Kreh's favor. Lefty was using an 8-weight prototype Sage rod. I don't know if this eventually made it into production, but it certainly performed well in

CAPTAIN JOE BLADOS

these conditions and in a matter of a few minutes, Paul was clamping a Boga Grip on the lower jaw of a striper that measured 28 inches.

When fishing deeper water, the presentation strategy changes because sinking lines come into play. A trip to Christmas Island some years back provides a vivid example of the adaptations I had to make when I decided to take a break from the flats to probe the depths for the likes of grouper, snapper and giant trevally. Christmas Island is one of those exotic places where you can experience incredible action on a variety of species both on and off the flats. The majority of anglers who visit this gem in the Pacific

to pulling an alarm in a fire house. The area is quickly vacated.

Lefty's fly landed about fifteen feet in front of the bass and Paul immediately shouted, "Strip, strip." It's comforting to know that regardless of who may be on the casting platform, guides will shout instructions with

confine themselves almost exclusively to the flats. That's understandable because in terms of numbers alone, you would be hard-pressed to locate a more abundant population of bonefish eager to whack your flies. Occasionally you can also expect to encounter members of the trevally clan in the shallows. However, I was anxious to take advantage of some of the other fishing opportunities that were available here. That meant venturing into deeper water where sinking lines are the order of the day.

A personable young fellow who made the trip to the island with a group of friends from Arizona had a puzzled look when he spotted one of my sinking-line outfits leaning against one of the vans that shuttled us to the boats. He told me that he was just getting started in fly-fishing the salt, had recently been to Baja and was frustrated when he tried to use a sinking line to catch yellowfin tuna. I informed him that there were large schools of yellowfin in close proximity to the island and invited him to join me that morning to give it a shot. In that all-too-familiar scenario when you're anxious to share a fishing experience with a friend, old or new, the tuna chose to elude us and after two fruitless hours of searching we came up empty-handed. I asked him if he wanted to return to the flats, when our guide, "Big Eddy" quickly interjected that there were plenty of fish to be had in the deeper water adjoining the coral reefs.

We motored over to a coral outcropping that looked like a giant-size version of the cauliflower my mother used to serve. I explained the sinking-line strategy to my new friend and handed him the rod, but he insisted that I cast first so he could have a clear picture of what was involved. The technique is not that difficult once you realize that unlike a floating line, a fly line that is designed to sink cannot simply be lifted from the surface. A sinking line does what its name indicates, it slips below the surface. So before you can execute a back cast, the line will have to be manipulated back to the surface. The way to do this is by means of a roll cast. However, prior to the roll cast, a portion of the fly line's weighted belly section will have to be stripped in. This is easy to gauge when using a shooting-head system due to the marked difference between the head section (the standard head is 30 feet in length) and the running line. All you do is strip the head back in to a point where the rear section is inside the rod's tiptop. Even if you are fishing in the dark, you will feel and hear the loop-to-loop connection between the running line and shooting head slide inside the rod tip. Now you can make the roll cast which will bring the remainder of the sinking-line head to the surface. With the line on the surface, immediately lift the line off the water and make the back cast. On the forward cast extend (shoot) a few feet of line so that the entire head section is outside the rod tip. Make one more back cast followed by the final forward cast.

"Big Eddy" was right about the abundant fish population near the coral head. I ran through the casting sequence described above, allowed the fly to sink to a mental count of 15, and then started stripping line. The fly may have been about half way up the water column when the line came tight in my hands. It's sort of like the sensation of an anchor grabbing bottom as you're playing out the rope. The speed with which the remaining line on deck raced through the guides and the tugging force I felt at the other end when I applied pressure to stay clear of the coral made it abundantly clear that I was connected to a very powerful adversary.

The contact was short lived. I was using one of my vintage Great Equalizer rods that I referred to in Chapter One. In the early 1970s this was the only big-game fly-rod commercially available, but I liked it so much that I was still fishing it some thirty years after its introduction. In terms of today's materials and design concepts this rod is somewhat dated, but it does a great job of handling heavy shooting heads (at the time I had on a 550-grain head) and it's a real stump puller. This was coupled to a Billy Pate Tarpon. When my friend first saw this outfit he remarked that it seemed really heavy but I assured him that we would not be overgunned. First of all, you need a substantial size outfit if you are going to throw heavy shooting heads. Secondly, when fishing waters like this, you never know what you'll run into and I didn't want to be caught short.

This point was driven home in dramatic fashion only scant seconds after I hooked up. Despite the rod's pulling power, I wasn't able to stop the fish from running to the coral and the 20-pound-test tippet shredded like sewing thread on a grinding wheel. "Big Eddy" had kind of a philosophical look. Apparently he had been through this many times before with hand lines. Before relinquishing the outfit to my friend with a fresh leader, he recommended that I forego the class tippet and fish with straight 100-pound test. I understood what he meant, but replied that we weren't trying to put food on the table and my friend was anxious to try the sinking-line setup regardless of the possible outcome.

As it turned out, he fared better than I. After a few muddled attempts, he got in synch with the casting rhythm and began throwing about 80 feet of line with ease. The sinking line is heavy and there is considerable inertia to overcome. His initial reaction was the common one. He was applying too much power to the rod. Instead, I made him slow the casting stroke and allow the line to load the rod. Once he developed a feel for the heavy

Improper line control can ruin your casts.

line, I told him to make a hard, sharp haul on the forward cast. What this does is greatly accelerate the speed with which the rod tip turns over. Line will shoot out with very little effort. Given the weight of the line and the manner in which it loads the rod, I told him not to be concerned with trying to form very tight loops. He quickly caught on and reached the stage where he began concentrating more on the actual fishing instead of the casting.

He laid out a nice cast about 20 feet from the coral and immediately started to retrieve his 7-inch version of a blue-and-white Deceiver. Nothing touched the fly and when he turned to me for an explanation, I told him that he was following a pattern common to those who were not experienced with sinking lines. With floating lines, we begin the retrieve soon after the fly lands on the water. However, doing so with sinking lines defeats their very purpose. You have to give the line time to sink. Here is where labels can be deceptive because even lines that are designated as "fast sinking" do not plummet into the depths anywhere near as fast as lead sinkers or metal lures. A fly-line's weight is not concentrated in a relatively small, confined mass so compared to lures and sinkers, its descent is gradual. The line's sink rate can be further compromised by the effects of water current and the type of fly being fished. It may not be readily apparent, but a large, heavily-dressed fly can be quite buoyant and will take more time to descend than a sparsely-tied pattern.

On his next cast, my friend waited before commencing his retrieve. I told him a good way to do this was a mental count that would give a good indication of how long it should take for the fly to reach the desired depth. For example, if you counted to 15 on the first cast and did not get a strike, on the next cast you might extend the count to 25. If you do get a strike, you have some assurance that a count of 25 is necessary to reach the fish's feeding zone.

I can't recall how long he waited, but I'll never forget his excited screech as the fly was stopped dead in its tracks somewhere in the depths below. I reminded him to apply as much pressure as he could to turn the fish from the razor-like coral and much to our delight he succeeded in doing so. The water is very clear in this part of the Pacific and it wasn't long before we could see flashes of silver-hued color circling beneath the skiff. Now the routine was pump and wind and in fairly short order the "Equalizer" once again lived up to its name and my new-found friend had his first blue star jack in the firm grip of Eddy's paddle-size hand. Sinking lines may not involve the finesse associated with their floating counterparts on shallow-water flats, but they play a major role in most facets of this sport and it's important to learn how to cast them.

A final aspect of the casting game that deserves consideration is the matter of distance. This is the one factor that is subject to the most discussion. It is also probably the most controversial. Few would argue that distance is unimportant. Instead it's the issue of how much line one should actually be able to cast in a given set of conditions. Interestingly, with the exception of those who cast in tournaments, distance seldom seems to be a major concern with conventional and spin fishermen. I guess that has something to do with the fact that they measure their casts in yards, not in feet. In fact, I would argue that the primary disadvantage fly-fishers face vis a vis their revolving spool and spinning counterparts, is the inability to make the long casts necessary to deliver the offering to the fish. I'll bet all my fishing gear that anyone who has logged time on the water chucking flies can recite frustrating instances where the fish were simply out of range.

In the early 1970s when I started to fly-fish in earnest, there were numerous times as a shore-bound angler when I couldn't reach the fish that were in front of me. One memorable experience took place at Penfield Reef near the township of Fairfield, Connecticut. I was fishing with my buddy John Posh who ranks as one of the Northeast's premier fly-fishers. John is one of those guys who maintains a low profile. You seldom see his name in print but he's been saltwater fly-fishing since the mid-1960s and few people know this section of Long Island Sound as well as John. John fishes from boats (he always has at least two ready to go) as well as the shore and on this beautiful fall afternoon, the tide was low, the bluefish and bass were obliging and we decided to wade the reef. At the time, fly-fishing the salt in the Northeast was still a rarity and we were the only two anglers in the water sporting fly rods. For the first half-hour or so I was wishing I had made a different choice of tackle. The anglers with spinning outfits were nailing fish on almost every cast. John and I flailed away but the breaking fish always seemed to be about 50 feet beyond our range. Our inability to draw strikes was bad enough. It was compounded by the ribbing we had to endure from the spin jockeys who were having a field day. Eventually the fish drove the bait closer to the reef and John hooked a nice bass. I had my first strike but was quickly cut off, the telltale sign of a bluefish.

A week later I experienced a similar situation, this time off Compo Beach in Westport, Connecticut. I was with Dick Alley, a Westport cop who spent his spare time fishing and writing about it for a recently established newspaper aptly titled, *The Fisherman*. The bluefish were on the beach, but Dick and I were having a difficult time reaching them with our fly gear. Thoroughly frustrated, Dick ran back to his car and grabbed a spinning outfit. I think he nailed about four fish before I finally connected with one on a popper. The blues would strike the fly-rod popper with the same ferocity they attacked the spinning lures. The only difference in the lopsided hookup ratio was purely a matter of casting distance. If I could have cast as far as the guys using spinning tackle, there is no doubt that I would have hooked just as many fish.

Restricted distance is not only a problem for the shore-bound fly-fisher. Over the years I can recall numerous instances where the inherent limitations of casting distance associated with fly tackle, significantly reduced my chances of catching fish. Yellowfin tuna proved particularly elusive. On some of my early trips down the Baja peninsula, my friends and I would chase yellowfin tuna in the Bay of Los Angeles from skiffs (these are called pangas in Mexico) that we rented from the local fishermen. The native fishermen down there really know their craft. They're great boat handlers and they always put us into fish. The only shortcoming was the bait problem. If you wanted to fish with it or use it as chum, you had to catch it yourself and this could be a time-consuming process. That was one reason we chose to fish mostly with artificials. Given the sheer power of these fish, the standard tackle arrangements consisted of stout conventional outfits. Trolling came into play primarily as a means of locating schools of tuna. Once we were into fish, it was a casting game and with 4/0 size reels and short, standup-style tuna rods designed primarily for bait-fishing, you had to be a proficient caster to fling the metal jigs out to the tuna. Because we didn't have bait, we were unable to draw the yellowfin close to the boat. With the exception of those times when we were lucky enough to slide into the midst of a feeding school, a minimum of 30- to 40-yard casts was necessary to reach the tuna. You can imagine what you're up against with fly tackle.

Indoors under ideal conditions, most good casters can hit that magical 100-foot mark. Tie on a weighted fly, stand on a pitching boat deck with your knees knocking up against the gunwales, mix in a stiff sea breeze, and the level of difficulty is multiplied many times over. That 100-foot cast suddenly diminishes considerably. Granted, you may seldom have to cast all that line, but the point remains, the angler who can make that 100-foot cast under perfect conditions will still be able to throw a relatively long line when the weather turns nasty. I know many anglers who wouldn't even try to fly-fish under adverse conditions, but if you are devoted to the sport, this is what you learn to deal with.

Generally in deep, open water, accuracy really isn't a problem and the manner in which the fly line is lifted from, or lands on, the surface is not that critical. In fact, where tuna are concerned, some surface disturbance can actually be beneficial. In my teens I had the opportunity to work on some of the commercial jack pole boats based in San Diego. I made brief reference to this fishery

surface with the poles. Somehow that seemed to arouse them. We were very limited in the distance we could throw the jig because the line was approximately the length of the pole, about 12 feet. Of course, that didn't matter because the tuna were literally at our feet. That is seldom the case when you're sport fishing. Like it or not, the plain fact is, that if you want to stand a chance of connecting with marauding schools of fish, regardless of the species, the distance you can throw the fly will often spell the difference between unparalleled excitement or dejected disappointment.

Many knowledgeable anglers argue that the majority of fish caught on fly are taken at distances of 65 feet or

Multiple hookups are common on long-range fly-fishing trips.

in Chapter One where I was discussing the subject of rods and what they're made to do. Here all you did with them was pull on fish. Albacore and yellowfin were the primary targets and we fished them with stout Calcutta poles and barb-less feathered jigs. In today's terms you could characterize this as a form of extreme fly-fishing, sans reels. Tuna were chummed to the boat with live bait and the fishermen stood in racks at water level where they flipped the jigs to the frenzied tuna. The jigs were maneuvered in a figure-eight pattern and if the tuna began to show any hesitation to strike, we splashed the

less. I don't know of anyone who has kept accurate statistics regarding this claim, but even assuming its veracity, there are a number of factors to consider. First of all, this may be due to the fact that most anglers cannot effectively cast much further than that. Practically every fly-fishing guide I know would agree with that assessment. Secondly, in flats fishing, which continues to be in the limelight of saltwater fly-fishing, speed and accuracy are more important than all-out distance. Here you cast to individual fish you can see, and if you are too far away, the guide can often pole you to within casting distance. The same applies when you are wading the shallows. You can either wait for the fish to swim closer, or shorten the distance by sneaking up on it. Nonetheless, there are many situations, including the flats where long casts are absolutely necessary.

I can recall another time at Christmas Island where two of the fellows in the group we were in initially made fun of the emphasis I placed on the importance of good casting technique and distance. It was the first full day of the trip and the deeper-water flat we were fishing did not require long presentations. Because of the waist-deep depth and a reduction in water clarity, the bonefish were not in their normal wary mode and were taking flies that were dropped only 20 to 30 feet away. Regardless of their experience level, everyone hooked a considerable number of fish and a very jovial mood permeated the dinner conversation later that evening. The following day however, saw a radical change, both in terms of fishing success and corresponding temperaments. Due to a tidal change and a different location, for the better part of the day, we were stalking bonefish in very shallow water often little more than ankle deep. Now it was an entirely different game. The bones were extremely wary and if you tried to narrow the gap by wading closer, the result was usually a sand cloud, the aftermath of a frightened bonefish suddenly vacating the area. Seventy- to 80-foot casts were usually necessary to avoid spooking the fish and the accomplished casters in the group actually enjoyed the added challenge. The two duffers who felt like heroes the day before, only managed a few hookups and they soon began to grumble. One of them even went so far as to accuse the guide of taking him to a place "that was fished out." That's a very familiar refrain you often hear when things aren't going well. I was glad one of his friends was closeby who informed him in no uncertain terms that it was his inability to cast that cost him fish, not the guide.

With the possible exception of billfish that have been teased close to the boat, when you move off the flats, most of the fishing will involve blind casting. When you cannot spot individual fish, but you know or hope they are in the area, the object is to cover as much water as possible. Similar to the situation of spin fishermen and conventional reel anglers, the greater the area you can work your fly through, the higher the probability that a fish will intercept your offering.

Although it wasn't my intention to do so at the time (I just wanted to catch fish), I demonstrated this principle on a long-range fly-fishing trip organized by Ed Rice. Ed was the main force behind the International Sportsmen's Expositions, which continue to produce some of the best fishing and hunting shows in the country. It was the fourth day of a ten-day outing that

CAPTAIN JOE BLADOS

already saw record catches of yellowfin and wahoo but we did have occasional slow periods when the ocean seemed almost devoid of life. When the action slowed down it was generally after the noon lunch and typically about half of the group would grab a little siesta time. I considered joining them, but the thought of another yellowfin pinning me over the rail was too much to resist. The morning's fishing had taken a toll on one of my 12-weight shooting-head outfits and rather than just go to another backup, I thought it best to take the extra time and rig a new head and leader.

The bow area was unoccupied so I took the spot and began making long, 80- to 100-foot casts off the starboard side. To allow the line time to sink, I would slowly walk back about mid ships and then commence jigging the fly by intermittently pulling on the line every other second. I would do this for a few minutes before stripping in the remainder of the line in preparation for the next cast. On my third or fourth cast I was just about to begin the final retrieve when the line became tight as a bowstring. A yellowfin grabbed the fly about 60 feet below and proceeded to rip off at least another 150 yards of line before I could begin the back-breaking task of muscling it from the depths. The situation was ideal because I was the only one hooked up and had the entire deck area to myself. Of course, the isolation was short-lived as others were anxious to get in on the action.

However, the bite remained slow except for myself and Trey Combs. Trey is an accomplished fly-fisher, but at the time, most of his experience was confined to fresh water (he wrote a definitive work on steelhead fishing). In the ensuing years Trey became absolutely enamored with saltwater fly-fishing. Big-game fly-fishing is his specialty and he has organized and fished on more long-range fly-fishing trips than anyone. Pick up a copy of his book, *Blue Water Fly-fishing*, and you will learn a great deal about this phase of the sport. Among other things, Trey is one of those people who are very observant. Most expert anglers are. They see what works and they adapt. Maybe it was all those years making long casts to steelhead in fast-moving rivers that tipped him off as to what was required. He understood what I was doing and quickly followed suit. As I recall, he hooked up on his first cast. Now we were following each other up and down the rail trying to make sure our lines did not tangle. We had company on deck, but for the next hour and a half we were the only ones tugging on tuna. It was the long casts in conjunction with the sinking lines that were producing strikes. Yellowfin were definitely in the area, but they were not concentrated and they were fairly deep. Long casts were necessary to cover the area and probe the depths. The short presentations simply did not pan out and the anglers who could not cast well basically went fishless. Their hook-ups were primarily confined to those periods when the tuna were in a feeding binge close to the boat. Think about it.

How many times can you recall where plug and lure fishermen deliberately try to shorten their casts?

More so than with other tackle modes, wind can be the fly-fisher's nemesis. You may like to think otherwise, but anytime you step outdoors, inevitably you will have to confront the breeze factor. Surf fishermen know this better than anyone. When fishing an open stretch of ocean from the beach, more often than not, the wind will be blowing directly into your face. Whether it's Manhattan Beach, California, or Montauk, New York, fishing the high surf often feels like you're standing behind a jet revving for takeoff. I can't think of a more inhospitable environment for fly-fishing. Yet we do it, and we love it.

The wind in your face definitely cuts down on distance. The wind at your side can be dangerous. If you're a right-handed caster, wind blowing to your right can drive the fly into you instead of the water. Many years ago I suffered that embarrassment casting for weakfish off New York's Shelter Island. I made what I thought was an excellent forward cast, but I never saw the fly land on the water. That's because it was stuck in my right ear. To be more precise, it pinned my ear to my head. I never felt it penetrate. I guess that's one of the advantages of sharp hooks. I've stuck myself a few times since then but for the most part I've learned to control the fly in the wind. One simple technique is to turn around and make the forward cast by means of a back-hand stroke. That way, the wind will blow the fly away from your body. Most fly-fishers seem to do it this way but another way to go is to tilt the rod on the forward cast so that the fly will pass safely to the right or left of your head. For example, a right-handed caster with the wind blowing in that direction would tilt the rod to the left. This will carry the fly safely in that direction. Lefty first demonstrated this to me on a bone-fishing trip in Belize. He saw me turning around to adjust for the wind and felt that it was too awkward, especially in flats fishing because you can easily lose sight of the target. From the standpoint of accuracy, tilting the rod is the best way to compensate for the wind but it does take practice and it's best done with just a leader and no fly. If you are new to this sport, the odds are that eventually you will hook yourself. I've even seen the master himself (Lefty) plant one in his derrière. It's one of the inevitable outcomes of this sport. The point is, you don't want to end up becoming a pincushion, and the only sure way to avoid this is practice.

CHAPTER 6

The Game Plan: Fly-Fishing Strategies

If I were writing a book on research methods, the present chapter would be entitled, Research Design. Here, where the interest is fly-fishing, I simply refer to it as the game plan, but it involves the same sort of basic concerns a scientist faces when planning a research project. Similar to a researcher faced with choosing a suitable methodology for studying a particular phenomenon, the fly-fisher must select a series of strategies designed to accomplish the ultimate objective of catching a particular fish. As we saw in the last chapter, casting is a key part of the strategy but there is considerably more involved. We also have to consider the issues involved in line control and retrieve techniques, hook setting and fish-fighting strategies.

Line Control and Retrieve Techniques

In common parlance, the word manipulator has negative connotations. Something most people would try to avoid. As fly-fishers however, manipulation is an integral part of our game. In a sense, when you make a cast you are manipulating the line as you choreograph its flight path through the air. In this chapter we'll look at another manifestation of line manipulation more properly referred to as line control. What most often comes to mind here is line retrieval or stripping techniques. But before we deal with these subjects, I want to mention the importance of controlling the line during the forward cast. This is accomplished by feathering the line in your line hand as it shoots through the guides on the final forward cast. Admittedly, this is something I do not do as often as I should. Most of my saltwater fly-fishing involves blind casting and I simply pick up the line in my free hand after the cast. However, there are situations where this puts you at a disadvantage

The author enjoying bonito action off the King Harbor breakwater in Redondo Beach.

because your line control is necessary as soon as the fly lands on the water. I learned this on my first trip to Bill Barnes' famed lodge, Casa Mar, nestled in a rainforest jungle on Costa Rica's northeast coast. Tarpon and snook get star billing in this piscatorial horn of plenty but there are a variety of other exotic species that will bow your rod and tighten your tippets. Lefty first told me about one of his favorites, the machaca. He refers to fishing for them as "machine gun bass bugging" and is so fond of it, that he often foregoes tarpon to tangle with these pit bulls of the jungle. The machaca have bodies similar to shad and they will get airborne when hooked. But unlike their North American look-a-likes, they are equipped with a devastating set of dentures. If you tried to lip one of these like a largemouth bass, you most certainly would come up short and considerably bloody.

Aside from the ensuing battle, a good deal of the fun fishing for machaca lies in the nature of the casting game. Machaca stay very close to the river bank where they lie in wait to ambush a variety of prey and food sources that fall into the water or are swept their way by the ever-present current. Since they do not have to move very far for a meal, the fly (primarily in the form of a popper) must be placed in tight to the structure where they live and feed. Just a few feet off will yield little more than arm exercise. The boat drifting along at three to four knots in the current, coupled with the irregular shoreline, makes for some very demanding casting. You need accuracy with the ability to constantly make adjustments for the variability in distance.

Machaca are voracious and determined feeders. The moment something lands on the water, be it a lizard, insect, or a cherry-shaped nut they are particularly fond of, the machaca attacks it immediately. This is what you can expect with a popper. If a machaca is in the area, the popper will disappear in a violent froth almost as soon as it hits the surface. The only way to be fully prepared to make an immediate hook set, is to cradle the line in your hand during the forward cast. By maintaining contact with the line as it shoots through your fingers, you are always in control and can react instantaneously if the popper is suddenly hit when it lands on the water. My first morning fishing I missed two or three initial strikes because I followed my normal routine and totally relinquished the line with my free hand. It may have only taken a second or two for me to reach for the line at the conclusion of the cast and tuck it under the index finger of my rod hand to commence the retrieve. But it was too late because the machaca had already struck and I was unable to react fast enough to set the hook. My guide Seurdo, just laughed and said, "you're too slow man, you have to be fast like the fish." Well Mother Nature didn't equip us with reflexes to match the speed of a machaca's (or any other fish for that matter) responses to a potential meal, but you can significantly speed up your reaction time by gingerly fingering the line during the cast.

Anytime you're throwing a surface offering like a popper where there is a chance that it might be struck as soon as it hits the water, you want to be ready by never losing contact with the line. I was lucky with the first

Sunrise on a tropical flat is a magical experience.

yellowfin tuna I took on a popper. I completely let go of the line during the cast and the tuna pounced on the popper before I could react. Fortunately, the football-shaped mass of muscle hit the popper with such force that it hooked itself. All I had to do was make sure the remainder of line on deck cleared the rod guides. Normally though, even when a fish aims to pounce on an offering with deadly determination, to effect a positive hook set, you'll have to strike back with the line.

The quickest way to do his is to make sure the line never leaves your hand.

Cradling the line in this manner is also good practice on the flats. In very shallow water the fly may have to be manipulated the moment it lands on the water. It may sink too rapidly falling below the fish's feeding zone, or the fish may overtake it before you can impart movement and then refuse to strike it. Striped bass and tarpon are notorious for refusing flies that are not in line with their cruising paths. The weight of the fly, the type of fly line and the current are factors that determine a fly's descent rate. Although it may seem very brief, the time span between a fly landing in the water and the beginning of its forward movement in the water during the retrieve also effects its depth level. Even a heavily weighted fly can be prevented from falling below a fish's cruising plane if the retrieve commences simultaneously with the fly landing on the surface. To do that, you'll need to have control of the line in your hand. When the fly is properly positioned, even a slight delay in the retrieve can cause a fish to rethink its decision to strike. I've had bonefish come up suddenly to a fly and then turn off because I wasn't able to quickly gather the line in my hand and impart action to it.

Recently Bob Popovics and I had the pleasure of fishing with Bob Clouser and his son Bobby on the Susquehanna River. Bob senior of course is the man behind the famed Clouser Minnow, a pattern he originally developed for his beloved smallmouth bass on the Susquehanna. In addition to the bass, there is another very interesting and sporting fishery Bob and his son have developed for their guiding clientele, stalking carp in the river shallows with fly gear. Carp, sometimes referred to as "coarse fish" by our English brethren, may lack the noble status of trout and bass, but sight-fishing for them in skinny water is every bit as challenging as bonefish on the flats. They grow considerably larger than most bonefish (10-pounders are not uncommon in the Susquehanna) and for all-out pulling power, they can hold their own with the likes of stripers and salmon. When they realize they've sucked in a fly instead of a tasty crayfish, they'll tear across the shallows leaving a wake of mud and small pebbles that reminds me of the debris trail created by high-speed race cars on the salt flats. However, the prerequisite for experiencing this thrill is a skillful presentation that incorporates both accuracy and proper line handling.

In a feeding scenario that is very similar to bonefish and redfish, carp will root out their prey by grubbing along the rock-strewn bottom. In the process of doing so, their tail fin and sometimes even their dorsal fin, is completely out of the water. Because they are focused on feeding, they tend to be less wary than when they are in a cruising mode, but they are not about to travel any distance to take a fly. You literally have to place it exactly where they are rooting which yields a zone about the

For many anglers, stalking fish in clear shallow water is the ultimate challenge.

size of a basketball. Hitting the target is only part of the game. Since the water is often only a foot or two deep, and the bottom is covered with stones, you have to immediately take control of the line as soon as the fly hits the water, otherwise it could easily become lodged in a crevice. The best way to do this is to cradle the line in your hand during the forward cast. That way, in the event you have overshot your mark by a few feet, the stripping process can proceed just as the fly lands on the water enabling you to guide it into the feeding zone with less chance of it fouling on the rocks. Even if the cast is right on target, it's best to have the line in your hand to be ready to react the instant the carp decides to devour the offering.

That is exactly what happened in one of those rare moments when the video camera is on trying to capture the action from the initial hookup to the final landing sequence. Popovics loves to shoot video almost as much as he loves to tie flies and fish and when Bobby Clouser pointed to a tail waving like a miniature flag about 40 feet to my right, Bob immediately turned his camera on it. I made the cast and the fly landed about a foot in front of the broomtail-shaped tail fin. This time I remembered to cradle the line in my hand during the cast and I began a slow strip as soon as the squirrel-hair Clouser hit the water. My hand did not travel more than a foot when the line came tight and began to slice through the water to my left. Bobby Clouser has the kind of voice that adds to the adrenaline level when he hits the high decibels, and the instant he saw the line straighten, he shouted, "You got him, you got him." I replay that pronouncement over and over in my mind, but at the time, I thought it might be a tad premature. I definitely hooked the carp, but as it was heading down river at a pace much faster than I could walk, the outcome of the contest was far from being settled.

With a stone-studded bottom interspersed with obstacles that run the gamut from discarded tires to broken tree limbs, the likelihood of a snagged line or frayed tippet was definitely cause for concern. In our favor, Bob and I were briefed by the Clousers well in advance of the trip, and we tailored our tackle choices according to their suggestions. We had 8-weight rods (I brought along a Thomas and Thomas Vector 3-piece and Bob had a new St. Croix) matched to Four-wide Islander reels and weight-forward floating lines. The tippets were 12-pound test and given all the potential hazards, I wouldn't recommend anything less. To help clear the structure, I held the rod high over my head, but there were still times when I could feel the line wedge between the stones as the carp plowed its way through riffles and over ledges. Fortunately, everything held together and after ten minutes or so of constant pressure, I managed to work the fish within range of Bobby's landing net. Judging by the girth of this carp, it seemed like it spent most of its life hanging around a Louisiana Bayou kitchen eating buckets of crayfish. In this case however, quite unlike most of its human counterparts, the body mass is measured in muscle. Carping with the Clousers gives new meaning to the Latin expression, *carpe diem* (seize the day) which I would rewrite as *carp diem*.

An integral part of line control involves the retrieve process after the cast is made. Of course in fly-fishing, this is a totally manual operation. I recall one of my non-fly-fishing friends being somewhat puzzled by the fact that the fly reel is not used to retrieve line for the purpose of manipulating the fly. It didn't quite make sense to him that a fly reel, (in this case he was referring to one of my costly, custom-crafted, saltwater models), came into play only during the fish-fighting phase, or when I wanted to put line back on the spool because I had quit fishing or casting. I tried to explain to him that for me at least, the sensation of the line in my hands was one of the major attractions of fly-fishing. As a kid I started fishing Long Island Sound with a hand line. That was all I could afford, but it brought me countless hours of pure enjoyment. There were no exotics in the lineup, but the antics of fluke, flounder and porgies chewing on my sand worms were telegraphed through my fingers and hands, giving rise to a special kind of stimulation that I could never seem to duplicate with spinning or conventional gear. Decades ago when I hooked my first fish on fly, I recaptured that feeling and it has remained my favorite angling mode ever since.

It may seem obvious, but the manner in which the line is handled governs both the fly's movement in the water as well as hook-setting effectiveness. A few summers back on Baja's Sea of Cortez, a young angler experienced a very poignant demonstration of these basics. It was a typical scorching July afternoon, and the action on dorado and billfish had shut off completely. I grew tired of watching the plastic skirts of the trolling lures break uninterrupted through the wavelets created by the boat's wake and decided to try an alternate method of teasing I learned years ago on one of my early trips down the peninsula. I asked the skipper to stop the boat so the mate and I could take in the three trolling lines. I rigged one of the few remaining live caballitos that were in the bait tank on a hookless harness and then instructed the captain to slow troll the bait by taking the boat in and out of gear. You don't cover as much ground this way, but if there is a predator game fish in the area, it is more likely to be aroused by a live offering than a fast-moving artificial.

I held the teasing outfit for about a half hour when I was suddenly jolted from drowsiness by a big, bull dorado that struck the bait before I could react. He tore it clean away from the 50-pound-test monofilament harness, something that was not supposed to happen. In most cases the fish just disappears with a free meal but sometimes they will linger in the hopes that something more will be available. With this in mind, I told the kid to cast the green and yellow Cotton Candy concoction I had tied the night before. The originator of this fly, Bob Popovics, was onboard with his video camera tight to his eye. Bob was the first to spot the dorado as it cruised across the stern corner about 40 feet from the boat. The 8-inch Candy hit the water and the dorado immediately swam to it but did not take it. It took me a second or two to realize that the kid had the fishing version of buck fever. He made a good cast but was so taken with the sight of the big dorado homing in on the fly that he just stood there with the line in his hand. I yelled to him to strip the fly.

When the Candy came to life, so did the dorado and it lit up like it had a massive injection of neon. This time when it came for the fly it never slowed its pace and pounced on it like a defensive back trying to put the hurt on a receiver. This was the first time Bob had ever seen any of his patterns in action on the offshore grounds and he let loose with the loud affirmation, "He's on!" Unfortunately, the excitement was short lived and Bob's triumphant shout was immediately followed by the sickening sound that monofilament makes when it's suddenly stretched beyond the breaking point. It's something like the sound of a 22-blank cartridge fired at the beginning of a track meet, only here it signals that the contest has come to an abrupt end. This kid was big and strong and had hands that could wrap around a football like octopus tentacles. The trouble was, he never allowed any line to slip through his fingers. Instead, he held on to it like it was a life rope and the 20 pound class tippet popped like frayed string on a brass yo-yo. If there were letter grades to be given, there would be an 'A' for the cast but he would have flunked the retrieving and hook-setting portions of the exam.

Fish, just like the folks who pursue them, are not alike. There are behavior differences both between and within species and this makes for tremendous variation in the ways fish approach and strike flies. The only hard and fast rule when it comes to imparting action to a fly is to learn to be flexible to accommodate the different conditions you're bound to encounter. As for the style of retrieve, it breaks down into two basic methods; the more traditional one-handed retrieve or a two-handed stripping technique. Each has its devotees, but most accomplished fly-fishers are equally adept using both styles.

There are a number of situations where I generally opt for a one-handed stripping style; when I'm using a deep stripping basket in the high surf, at times when I'm standing on a boat's casting platform and generally when I'm working surface poppers. Particularly in West Coast style surf fishing where you are standing on a beach facing the open ocean, you can expect large waves and a strong undertow. Strictly speaking, you are wading, but in reality it is neither practical nor prudent to venture out beyond the point where the water rushes to your shins. In conditions like this I use a deep-model stripping basket (these will be discussed in more detail in the next chapter) that rides alongside my left hip. By stripping line with my left hand, the line falls neatly into the basket by my side.

Despite the fact that they are designed for fly-fishing, working from a flats skiff with a front deck that is flush to the gunwales can be a problem if it's windy because line will blow off the deck. Especially for inexperienced fly-fishers, this can be frustrating as hell because most of the time they are not aware of what's happening. The angler is focused on fishing and is totally unaware of what is going on with the line as it is being retrieved. They assume it will be lying at their feet, but when they try to execute the next cast, they're in for a rude surprise. Even if the boat is not drifting, it is very difficult to make a cast with a portion of the line in the water.

Of course, one way to prevent this is to wear a stripping basket. A second alternative is to stand near the rear side of the platform and use a single-handed stripping motion directing the line to fall on the deck where it won't be blown over the side. This is a technique I used extensively last season fishing the flats and the rips off the north shore of Long Island with Joe Blados. Joe has a beautiful, new, 21-foot Maverick flats skiff that is tailor made for fly-fishing. However, particularly when fishing the rips you can expect wind, and if you're not wearing a basket, line will blow off the casting platform. Initially, my girlfriend at the time who was just learning to fly-fish, had a terrible time. Joe would put her on a school of blitzing bluefish and if she didn't connect on the first cast, things would go from bad to worse. She would strip line furiously but never pay attention to where the line was falling. Most of the time it was overboard and she couldn't make an effective cast to get the fly to the breaking blues. After missing several ideal opportunities, she became attentive to where she was standing and was careful to strip the line so that it would land flush on the deck below the casting platform. My only problem now is coaxing her to relinquish the spot so I can have a go at the action.

I also tend to favor a single-hand retrieve when I want to create a lot of surface commotion fishing poppers. If there is a popper heaven, I think I found it at Midway Island. The giant trevally and amber jack love surface offerings and it seems the more disturbance you create, the more excited they get. Popovics' flat-faced popper aptly labeled, Bob's Banger, was the hot ticket because it pushed water like a tug boat in reverse. But to get the most out of the popper, I used a series of sharp, single-handed tugs on the line that caused the Banger to thrash the surface like kids splashing in a pool. Both the amber jack and trevally hit it with equal vengeance but I will never forget one momentous strike when an amber

Crashing bait alongside a submerged jetty—a sure sign of action.

jack with the proportions of a mini sub shot up from the depths and crashed on the Banger. The last remaining image was the surface froth that looked like the foam in a brewer's vat. Neither the amber jack nor Banger were ever seen again.

Up until about a year ago, I didn't think it was possible to work a popper effectively using a hand-over-hand retrieve. Popovics changed all that. One late afternoon we were fishing off Martha's Vineyard's famed Lobsterville Beach. Stripers were our principal target and we were using Clear Intermediate fly lines on 9-weight rods. As often happens at Lobsterville, both bass and bluefish would periodically bust the surface in their pursuit of sand eels that they ambushed in tight to the beach. In an effort to "match the hatch," we were using sand eel patterns. They worked fine on the

gluttonous blues who typically will strike just about anything when they're in a feeding spree, but the bass were a lot more selective and we weren't hooking any. After a fruitless half-hour with the stripers Bob, who was fishing about 50 feet to my left, suggested we try poppers. I shouted back that I didn't think they would work effectively on the slow-sinking lines we were using. His reply was, "tie one on and I'll show you how I work it."

We both had dishpan-size stripping baskets in front of our waists which are very convenient when you employ a two-handed retrieve because the line falls directly into the basket below your hands. To my surprise, Bob continued with his two-handed retrieve, but to achieve a maximum level of surface disturbance, he made two modifications. Instead of pointing the rod tip directly at the water, he positioned the rod between his arm and torso so that the tip was pointed at a slight angle above the surface. This helps prevent the line from pulling the popper into the water. Secondly, his normal hand-over-hand retrieve was altered in such a manner that when he grasped the line in his left hand, rather than pulling straight back, he swept his hand upward. The upward tug keeps the popper riding high on the surface and imparts the same kind of action that you normally achieve with a floating line. This may not seem like a major innovation, but it is a very important technique because you no longer have to rely exclusively on floating lines to fish poppers. It's a definite advantage when you don't have the luxury of an additional outfit or for those times when changing lines is too time-consuming or inconvenient.

Obviously the rate at which the fly moves is governed by how fast you strip the line and although it is by no means limited to this application, I imagine the two-handed retrieve first came into play as a means of speeding the fly's pace through the water. Of course, what you always have to bear in mind is the fact that Mother Nature equipped her finned creations with lightning-quick reaction time. Whether it's walleye or wahoo, if the predator wants your offering, you cannot retrieve fast enough to prevent it from taking it. There are many situations however, where a fly's speed can be critical in drawing a strike. Wahoo are a prime example. As of this writing, there are still relatively few fly-fishers who can lay claim to taking one of these speedsters on fly. I believe Stu Apte was one of the first to do so. I know that when he and I made a long-range fly-fishing trip together back in the mid-nineties, we were the only ones on the boat who had taken wahoo. Since then, some remarkable catches have been made and most have taken place from the decks of the long-range boats based in San Diego.

Prior to my first wahoo on fly in 1987, I had a decade of experience taking these high-speed scalpels on conventional gear. The most fun was casting to them with metal jigs and the name of the game was speed. A rapid retrieve was accorded such high priority that special gear kits designed to increase the reel's gear ratio were commonplace on the long-range boats. Generally, the faster you could move the jig through the water, the better the chances of a wahoo nailing it, and having a "hoo" explode out of the water and dive bomb your jig is an unforgettable experience.

Naturally, when I began fly-fishing for wahoo on these trips in the early 70s, I felt it imperative to burn the fly through the water as fast as I could and a two-handed retrieve was my standard practice. And it brought results. Even though I never landed a wahoo on fly on those early trips, I had a number of close encounters and they all rank as some of the most memorable experiences in my fly-fishing career. The largest wahoo I ever connected with was on the fly rod. The two deckhands who stood beside me and saw the fish's flanks silhouetted against the background of Socorro Island as it skyrocketed from the surface both thought it would hit the 100-pound mark. Apparently, the single-strand wire had a kink in it because it broke and the fish swam off with a 6-inch purple-and-black Deceiver trailing from the side of its lower jaw.

My first fly-rod wahoo came from Costa Rica's Cano Island. I was skiff fishing and having a great time catching school size yellowfin. My guide hooked a wahoo on conventional tackle and we decided to troll a plastic skirt to see if we could draw one to within casting range of the boat. It's been my experience that wahoo do not travel in large schools like their close cousins the tuna, but where there is one, there are usually others in the wolf pack cruising for a meal. We used an 80-pound outfit for the trolling setup to try and control a hooked fish before it made off with too much line. My young guide knew how to handle tackle and soon after a wahoo struck the plastic-skirted trolling lure, he had it thrashing in the skiff's wake. I put the outboard in neutral and made a cast while the boat was still sliding forward. To take advantage of the skiff's forward progress, I stripped the line hand over hand the instant the streamer hit the water. The skiff was barely moving but the slight forward drift enhanced the fly's speed on the retrieve and a wahoo came slashing in on the streamer. I'm convinced that the fly's quickened pace drew the wahoo's interest.

However, there are no absolutes in this game and as more fly-fishers began to encounter wahoo on the long-range trips, it became evident that one of the most effective ways to elicit a strike was to simply allow the fly to drift in the current behind the boat. The key to this technique is the live bait that is used as chum. Wahoo are ravenous feeders and when they home in on a bait, it's like a missile locking on to a target. There is no baitfish in the ocean that can outrun them. Similar to bluefish in this respect, when wahoo blitz through a ball of bait, the scene is pure carnage. The baitfish that are not devoured whole on the initial attack suffer an even crueler fate. Their demise is sealed, but death comes more slowly as some are cut in half, while others are slashed and

Bill Barnes trying to maneuver a large striped marlin away from the boat's props.

stunned. The water is littered with silver scales that glitter like the synthetic snow in crystal balls. Those that are able, make a feeble attempt to remain swimming, but the effort is fruitless and they flounder like leaves tumbling in the current. Having been programmed into their genetic script over eons of time, wahoo seem self-assured about the inevitable outcome of the assault. The wounded and decapitated are there for the taking and wahoo shift into a more leisurely mode where they casually pick off the remains. It is this mop up operation that fly-fishers on the long-range trips have learned to adapt to. By allowing the fly to drift back in the chum, it simulates the characteristics of injured bait and wahoo go for it like it was another tasty morsel.

This same tactic also works for shark and tuna. In their world, nature equipped them to play the part of high-speed predator. Their principal feeding mode consists of hunting and devouring prey on the run. However, despite the elegance of nature's design, the kills are not always clean. And since nourishment is never a sure thing, nothing is wasted and the hunter lingers to feed on the leftovers. This is part of their survival script. The predator role is a flexible one and food sources in the form of chum present an opportunity they can seldom afford to ignore. Fly-fishers play their part by presenting an offering that resembles the chum in both appearance and movement.

The first concern is a relatively easy one. All you have to do is select a fly that simulates the chum. If cut bait in the form of mackerel or bonito is used to attract sharks, a simple creation consisting of red marabou palmered around a hook shank will generally provide a convincing simulation. It is the second part of the equation that fly-fishers sometimes overlook. The key to any presentation is to make it appear convincing. You want the fly to blend in with the natural order of the prevailing set of conditions. For example, if a shark or tuna were initially attracted by a rapidly moving teaser, to induce a strike it may be necessary to retrieve the fly as quickly as possible. On the other hand, if fish are leisurely picking off morsels in a chum slick, the most natural presentation is to simply drift the fly back in the slick.

All this sounds easy enough, but even with a plentiful supply of chum, the quarry often do not respond the way you want them to. Fishing sharks is a good example. When most people think of sharks, the Hollywood-induced image that is likely to come to mind is a fearsome creature with an insatiable appetite that indiscriminately devours everything in its path. There are times when this isn't far from the truth. On a long-range trip to Hurricane Bank, a remote underwater ledge that lies a couple of hundred miles off the southern tip of Baja, we were forced to leave the area because of sharks. No one could make an accurate identification of the particular species. All I can report is that they were large (approximately 8 to 12 feet in length), extremely aggressive, and very fast. It was a big disappointment because the Bank was a 20-hour run from where we

were situated the day before and the wahoo fishing was something you dream about. Every jig that hit the water was instantly attacked. The only trouble was, no one managed to bring one intact to the boat. I don't know if scientists run time trials to make estimates of how fast various species can swim through the water, but for my money nothing beats a wahoo.

Personally, I have never hooked anything that can match it for all-out speed. They light out so fast that the line literally hisses as it slices through the water creating a roostertail like a jet-boat racer. Granted that its normal speed might be slightly compromised when it's pulling against a line with drag pressure, but I still find it incredible that these sharks were able to intercept them. If you were lucky, you brought in a mangled carcass. Most anglers were left with limp lines blowing in the sea breeze. A Hollywood producer would love this kind of action.

Midway Island also showed me the nasty side of sharks. The first day out the guide finished off a cold drink and threw the can overboard. I was about to say something about littering when he told me to keep my eyes on the can. Probably not more than 10 seconds elapsed, when a large copper-colored shark swam by and snatched it from the surface.

This was the first place I had ever cast a fly to a shark where it simply swam up and ate it with no added inducement from any chum. It occurred one morning when we decided to run offshore in search of billfish and yellowfin tuna. We found the latter with little difficulty, unfortunately so did the sharks. My first hookup was with a yellowfin that was easily in the hundred-pound class. I realize that when anglers estimate the size of fish they never actually measure or weigh, the figures are often grossly disproportionate. But I have been eyeballing tuna for the better part of 40 years, and I clearly saw the fish boil on the fly not more than 20 feet behind the stern. The day before, in the same area, a trio of anglers using conventional big-game tackle landed yellowfin ranging from 40 to 160 pounds and the skipper who had an even better view on the fly bridge, confirmed that this fish was definitely in the triple digit class. Tackle-wise, I was prepared for the big boys. The lightest outfit I packed for Midway was a 12-weight, and when I went offshore, I rigged a 14-weight Thomas and Thomas Horizon rod with a Billy Pate Bluefin reel. To maximize the backing capacity (there was over 400 yards of 30-pound Dacron), I used a 25-foot sinking head that I cut from a length of Scientific Anglers 750-grain Deep Water Express.

As soon as I hooked this brute, I knew I was going to be in it for the long haul and I asked the mate to get me my fighting belt. The tuna sounded like a concrete safe heading for the bottom and for a time I was concerned that I was going to run out of line. It finally settled in the depths and I began the grueling task of trying to regain line. About 20 minutes elapsed before I was able to take a few cranks on the reel handle. My friend Mike thought I was beginning to win the contest, but I knew better. Tuna this size do not give up so easily. There was only one other answer. The telltale thumps telegraphed on the rod told me that the tuna was losing weight by the seconds. The captain looked down from the bridge and spoke the one word that was going through my mind, "Shark." Soon all the pressure was gone and I wound back all the line with a leader that was severed cleanly in half. We moved a mile or so and encountered another school of yellowfin.

These tuna were considerably smaller, in the 18- to 30-pound class, but we never managed to get any to the boat. The sharks took every one. Frustrated at not being able to land any, I decided to at least try for the sharks. It was very easy. I rigged a 4/0 sailfish streamer with 6 inches of 60-pound single-strand wire and made a short cast about 40 feet off the stern corner. A single-handed retrieve that pulled the fly along in foot-long increments caught one of the shark's attention and it casually swam over and took the fly. I had a good hook set in the corner section of its jaw and after it made off with about 100 yards of line, I was able to work it back to the boat where the mate deftly cut the wire inches from its deadly jaws.

This all sounds rather matter of fact, but I have also encountered situations where sharks and tuna were maddeningly discriminating and would steadfastly refuse the fly, choosing instead to dine on the chum that was being dispensed. Even blue sharks that are noted for their opportunistic scavenging (they earned the moniker, "blue whaler" for their propensity to dine on floating blue whales that had been harpooned) can be very picky when they're feeding in a chum slick. I have drifted a fly in the slick for as long as a half-hour before a blue would finally decide to eat it like it was another floating morsel breaking loose from the chum container. The same scenario was repeated with yellowfin using live anchovies or "fresh dead" baits as chum. The tuna would shoot up from the surface and methodically pick off every bait tossed over the side, but ignore the fly like a kid who wanted the ice cream, not the vegetables. However, with dead baits there is a technique that sometimes induces a

strike. It has nothing to do with the retrieve. Instead it's a function of the manner in which the fly is presented. Sometimes when the bait is thrown hard causing it to strike the surface with a loud smack, the tuna's arousal coefficient is increased and they take the chum in a more aggressive manner. If you can establish a pattern throwing three or four baits in this manner at 5-second intervals and then substitute the fly as the final offering, the tuna will frequently go for the fly like it was another bait. You can do the same with makos, only here the chum consists of 2-inch chunks of fresh bonito or mackerel. There is really no retrieve involved, but you do want to be prepared for a strike the instant the fly hits the water making this another instance where the line should be feathered in the free hand during the forward cast.

Generally, for those situations where I do want to retrieve the fly, I opt for the two-handed method regardless of how fast I want it to move through the water. This is one application where I'm convinced that two hands are better than one. Two hands afford better control of the line simply because one hand is always in contact with the line. This makes it possible to impart an infinite variety of movements to the fly. Fast starts, accelerated streaks, intermittent pauses and slow crawls are all easily choreographed using the hand-over-hand retrieve.

Finally, in the double-handed approach, because the line is not being drawn across your finger, line burns caused by abrasive line surfaces are no longer a problem. Today's line finishes are the best ever but often they pick up microscopic pieces of grit. In the process of constantly pulling it across your finger, a cutting action is created similar to the effect of exposing your skin to a sander. Fishing the beaches on the Caribbean side of Costa Rica posed a particular problem in this respect. The black sand from ancient volcanic flows is beautiful to look at, but when it clings to the fly line it acts like an emory board and the finger on your stripping hand pays the price. You can offset this by taping fingers or wearing a glove. I have done both, but I feel my ability to monitor the line is compromised. Personally, I find the hand-over-hand stripping technique to be the best alternative.

Setting the Hook

In many instances, particularly with hard-mouthed saltwater species, I've found that I can strike a fish more effectively with two hands on the line. This became clear to me years ago when I fished Casa Blanca in Mexico's Ascension Bay. The flats fishing there can be phenomenal, but I'm always open to trying something different. I had three days of very productive fly-fishing for bonefish and baby tarpon, when my guide's brother asked if I wanted to go fishing with him after hours. His family was having a birthday celebration for one of the daughters and they wanted fresh fish for the fiesta. He made it clear that we would be bait fishing and I should leave the fly gear at the lodge. The tackle consisted of simple hand lines that brought back memories of my youth. It was almost 40 years since I had fished this way, but it didn't take long before I was almost keeping pace with my new friend. I noticed that he was striking the yellowtail snapper with two hands on the line. In my best Spanish I asked why he did it this way and his simple reply was, "es mejor," it's better. I didn't need any further explanation because he almost never missed a strike.

When you observe people fishing for food, as is often the case in Third World countries, hand lines are often

BILL BARNES

It appears as if the angler has yanked this tarpon from the water. That of course is not the case. His hand is placed too far up the rod and he should be pointing the rod at the fish (bowing) to create slack in the line.

the preferred mode of hook and line fishing. No doubt this is in large part due to the scant investment that is required, but more is involved than basic economics. I have been in many areas in Mexico and Central America where the locals have access to good tackle, but often choose to forego rod-and-reel combinations when they fish to put food on the table. This is because hand lines are often the most functional. There are no rods and reels to fail and the hook-setting procedure is most effective when the line is manipulated directly in one's hands when the line comes tight directly in your hands.

The thrill of the experience aside, striking the fish with the line generally is the most effective way of assuring a positive hook set because the path of the opposing force is direct and uninterrupted. Striking the fish with the rod may work on trout streams, but for most situations it's

not the way to go. When you see someone repeatedly strike back with the rod the thought that probably first comes to mind is that the angler is trying to free the hook from some obstacle like a bush, trees or a rock and that is often precisely the case. Strangely enough, this is how some fly-fishers (usually the inexperienced) try and set a hook. It's not very effective.

Bill Barnes taught me this many years ago tarpon fishing at his lodge in Costa Rica. Tarpon are notoriously difficult to hook. They have a series of bony plates in their mouth and attempting to plant a hook in their jaw has been compared to trying to stick a hook in a stone wall. It ain't easy. After watching me blow two fish in a backwater tributary about 10 miles down river from the lodge, Bill instructed me to forget about the rod. I was using a hand-over-hand retrieve, but when a tarpon hit, I would attempt to strike with the line hand, remove the rod from under my arm and then strike again, this time sweeping the rod to my right. On my next try, I followed his instructions and continued to strip line until I felt it come tight in my hands.

Jeffery Cardenas, one of the Keys' most experienced tarpon fishermen, likens this process to hammering a nail. A carpenter wouldn't try to drive a nail into a board with one swing of the hammer and anglers shouldn't attempt to stick a tarpon on the first strike. When you first feel resistance, it signals that the fly is in the tarpon's mouth, but that does not necessarily mean that the hook is planted. Continue to strip line until you feel very firm resistance. Then strike by pulling directly back on the line with your hands. This may cause the fish to immediately bolt, but if it doesn't, strike again, two to three times if possible. I managed two firm jabs and the fish headed for the heavens.

It's difficult to maintain composure when 100-plus pounds of contorting muscle shoots from the surface like a Polaris missile, but this is no time to lose your cool. When the fish clears the water it's important to give a little slack to help prevent the fish from throwing the hook. The standard term for this move is bowing, but what you're actually doing is reaching forward with the rod. This reduces the tension on the line which helps the hook stay planted even through a series of violent head shakes that can feel like your rod tip is stuck in a paint-mixing machine. Generally you can anticipate the fish's jump as the line begins to angle upward. In fact, this is the signal that I used to alert Bill who was standing ready with the camera trying to get jump shots. I would yell, "Here he comes," and Bill would fire the motor drive like one of those paparazzi photographers who has a celebrity in sight. This particular tarpon was very acrobatic and I think Bill burned up a roll of film just on the jumps. When I finally got it alongside the boat he was busy changing film and the battle was prolonged another five minutes before he was finally able to grab the leader in preparation for the release.

I have been using this striking technique ever since and I'm convinced that my percentage of boated tarpon is much higher than if I tried to rely primarily on the rod. Even with a single-handed retrieve, if you strike with the line, you will achieve more positive hook sets than if you strike with the rod. Regardless of the species, lower the rod tip and point it in the direction of the fish. Then use the line to plant the hook.

path. What you want to do is maintain tension on the line. If the line gets tight, it means the fish has the fly, and often I do not even pull back on the line. Instead, I hold onto it briefly until I feel an increase in the tension. The instant the bonefish begins to take off, allow the line to slip through your hand and enjoy the action. If you feel that telltale tap but the line doesn't get taut, it means that the fish does not have control of the fly. They are not perfect and from time to time they do miss their targets. But like a cat playing with a mouse, they are not likely to allow what they interpret as a food source travel very far. If they are not totally incapacitated, most prey at this point will keep moving in an effort to avoid capture. To simulate this, it's important to keep stripping the line. By pulling back on the rod when you first feel the fish, you cannot maintain the stripping sequence and more than likely the fish will lose interest.

Billfish are a world apart from bonefish, but the principles of line manipulation in relation to the strike remain basically the same. In the case of bonefish however, if you miss a strike, the chances are usually

Proper technique: the rod is pointed directly at the airborne tarpon.

Fish, like people, do not all eat in the same manner. Of course, with the former it's biology, not culture, that plays the dominant role in determining how the creature takes in its food sources. Thus, different species of fish may vary considerably in the way they take a fly, but by using your hands, you can adjust to the variation. With bonefish for example, the sensation can sometimes be rather subtle. You're stripping in the fly and you feel what can best be described as a brief tick in the line. Actually this is a momentary interruption in the fly's forward movement when a bonefish first pecks at the offering. If you react by jerking the rod upward at this point, you're likely to end up feeling like one (a jerk) because all you've done is swept the fly from the fish's

good that you will have multiple opportunities with other fish. Billfish are typically not as plentiful. As an experienced marlin fisherman friend of mine describes the game, "billfishing means big bills and few fish." So if you blow it with a sailfish, or worse yet a marlin, your chances for another shot may be few and far between.

A bluewater, fly-fishing clinic I conducted at Baja's East Cape back in the summer of '95 provides a dramatic example of missed opportunities with billfish. Like other phases of the sport, striking fish takes practice. But unless you spend a great deal of time on the water actually presenting flies to fish, the opportunity to practice is very limited. In all of my fly-fishing classes I try to simulate the experience of a fish taking a fly by playing the part of a fish. The student has a fully rigged outfit (sans fly) and I stand about 20 feet away with the leader in my hand. I have the student look downward so they cannot see me and then I tell them to begin stripping line. After several seconds I do my part by tightening the line in my hand so they can feel the initial strike. Then slowly at first, I start to make off with the line. The drill is repeated as often as necessary to enable the student to develop a feel for what's happening and how they should react. This is not unlike a baseball player taking batting practice from a pitching machine. It's not the same as facing a live pitcher in a real game, but you have to start somewhere and it's much better to experience failures and mishaps in practice sessions where there's really nothing at stake except maybe your ego.

I remember trying to explain all this to one of the students who was an orthopedic surgeon from San Diego. Drawing on my early experience as a pre-med student, I used the analogy with medicine. Long before you ever get to work on a live patient, you put in years of practice with varied subjects like frogs, dogfish, cats and human cadavers. Happily, the training is nowhere near as rigorous in fly-fishing. For my own tastes, I find the latter a lot more fun and the consequences of a mishap, disheartening though it may be, are nowhere near as disastrous.

Each of the eight participants in this five-day clinic had some fly-fishing experience, but no one had ever fished for bluewater species. To give them some advance preparation, the first day was spent on the beach in front of the lodge (we were staying at Rancho Buena Vista), where I discussed and demonstrated the basics of billfishing. The remaining four days I was on the water with each of the students who fished in pairs. Two of the fellows already had aspirations of getting into the record book and I had to diplomatically explain that given their lack of experience, this was somewhat premature. At least they were somewhat appeased when I covered the IGFA regulations needed to qualify for a record catch. In addition to the tackle and leader requirements, I emphasized that the boat must be in neutral when the cast is made. The presentation and striking techniques I covered had all been well established years before on the offshore grounds. The basic strategy was as follows:

When we reached the fishing grounds, which at the time were about eight miles off shore, the three teaser lines were set in the water. I had the angler whose turn it was to fish, strip out a 25-foot head cut from a Ric ST15 and 30-foot of running line. To help prevent costly tangles, the line was carefully stored in a plastic bucket in the stern corner. Even in the fish-rich waters of Baja, waiting for a sail or marlin to pop up behind one of the teasers can be agonizingly slow and cradling a 12- to 14-weight outfit in your hands is tiring. A better alternative is to lay the rod on deck alongside the gunwale on the side of the boat from where the angler will make the cast. Placing a towel under the reel will prevent it from sliding around on deck. Initially the drag should be set at approximately 1/2 of the breaking strength of the class tippet. The outfits were rigged with 20-pound-class tippets and using a hand scale, the drags were set in the range of 3 to 5 pounds. When a fish was first sighted behind a teaser, I had the angler pick up the outfit and grasp the fly (in this case we were using offshore poppers that I made for the school) at the bend of the hook between the thumb and forefinger. You want the 4/0 hook in the fish, not your finger. As the fish was being drawn closer to the boat, I directed the angler to let out about 20 feet of line behind the transom. When the person manipulating the teaser feels that the fish is sufficiently aroused and in casting range of the angler, the angler is told to make the cast. Since the fly is already dangling in the water, in most cases all the angler has to do is lift it from the water, make a back cast and one forward cast to the fish. With sailfish or marlin, the object is to place the fly about 5 to 6 feet to one side of the fish. This way, the fish must turn almost 90 degrees to take the fly, increasing the chance of hooking it in the corner of the mouth. It's almost impossible to hook a billfish coming straight at the fly because the beak is very hard. So is their lower lip in front. Making the fish turn to take the fly, increases your chances of hooking it in the soft corner of its mouth. The tongue and top portion of the mouth also affords good hooking potential.

The stripping technique depends on the reaction of the fish. Some of the professional captains I know who regularly fish the Pacific side of Costa Rica, advise their anglers to let the popper sit on top of the water without imparting any stripping action. They feel the commotion of the half-dollar size popper splashing down on the surface is all it takes to get the sail's or marlin's attention. However, be prepared for the fact that each encounter may be different and there are times when it's advisable to strip the fly in rapid sequences. If the fish doesn't respond on the first or second presentation, a teaser may have to be re-employed to reestablish the fish's attention.

When the fish does grab the fly, the accepted practice is to strip the line until you feel it come tight. Most experienced bluewater fly-fishers use a single-handed strip. A right-handed angler will strike by pulling back on the line with the left hand while simultaneously sweeping the rod to the right. Using both hands in this manner helps achieve maximum penetrating force without over-stressing the leader. It is important to strike with the rod sideways and not straight up. The reason for this is that it gives you a chance to recover in the event the fish runs directly toward the boat. With the rod pointed up in the air, you are away from the plane of the fish and will not be able to get the line tight again quickly.

This is what happened to my surgeon student. It was the third morning of the school and I was on the boat with him and his partner. The doctor had drawn the lot to have the first chance at a fish and he was really pumped for the opportunity. Sailfish were the expected quarry, but after an hour and a half of uneventful trolling, I spotted a pair of striped marlin finning on the surface off the port side of the boat. It was obvious that the captain had his eyes on them also, because the boat began to turn into position simultaneously when I yelled, "Marlin!" The drill went exactly as planned. The two unoccupied teaser lines were quickly brought in, the mate had drawn one of the marlin to the starboard line and the doc was ready with the popper bouncing gingerly in the wake. The marlin was lit up like a Christmas display in Rockefeller Center and when I told him to make the cast, he made a textbook-perfect presentation. The thoroughly aroused marlin heard the splash, veered toward the popper and pounced on it like a fullback on a fumble. The doc waited for the fish to turn and we could see the popper hanging in the corner of its jaw like an over-sized cotton wad. I yelled for him to strike and this is when he made the fatal mistake. He swung back with the rod like he was trying to poke the clouds but only succeeded in tearing the popper from the fish's mouth. It floated innocently on the surface and the doctor looked like he lost his first patient. What made him all the more frustrated was the fact that he knew what he was supposed to do. All he could say was, "I lost my cool," and that's easy to do when you have a hundred-plus-pound marlin tearing off with your fly. Striking a fish with the rod swept upward is a very common mistake and fly-fishers miss a lot of fish that way. And once it develops into a habit, it is not easy to break. I have a friend who is a very experienced angler, taking trips to the Keys and other exotic locales at least six times a year. He lands a considerable number of fish but acknowledges that he muffs way too many strikes simply because he has a difficult time disciplining himself to strike with the line.

It was almost exactly a year after the Baja school when I made my next trip down the Mexican peninsula, this time with a group of buddies all of whom are very accomplished fly-fishers. If you have ever taken a friend to one of your favorite fishing spots, you know the extra measure of anxiety you feel if the action isn't up to expectations. With five close friends, some of whom traveled all the way from the East Coast, my coefficient of concern was nearing the edge of the chart. Fortunately, the billfish started to turn on the last two days of the trip and three of the guys got shots at striped marlin. On the last day out, I shared a boat with Mike Wolverton. Mike is one of those guys who can do it all. Living in Idaho, trout streams are as familiar to him as daily commute routes and he's logged more saltwater time than many coast-bound locals.

I drew the first casting turn and Mike had the task of handling the principal teaser. We were trolling plastic-skirted Zucker marlin lures that were spiced with foot-long strips of dorado belly. When a sail or marlin clamps down on the lure, a strip bait provides a taste of the real thing which can significantly enhance the fish's arousal level. We just finished eating a pair of delicious bean-and-egg burritos when Mike remarked that he hoped the marlin would find the teasers equally as tasty. The fish gods were listening because about 15 minutes later we saw a dorsal fin pierce the water like the tip of a sub's periscope. Dream-like drowsiness was instantly transformed into an adrenaline rush. Mike manned the teaser rod and within seconds the marlin was in casting range, its vertical stripes glowing like neon bars. I was using his 14-weight Sage rod with a Billy Pate Bluefin reel. At the business end of the leader was my blue-and-white, tandem hook, Big Game Fly. Mike had the fish so crazy, he had a difficult time pulling the belly strip teaser away from it. When he finally managed to tear it away, I substituted the fly and the marlin turned on it instantly. The hook placement was perfect, right in the corner of the jaw. I struck the fish with several sharp jabs and we all let out shouts of jubilation as it headed off for mainland Mexico. The fish took about 75 yards of line when everything suddenly went limp. Thinking that the marlin made a sudden turn, I cranked on the reel handle as fast as I could, but the line never got tight again. I don't know if one or both of the hooks penetrated the fish. The take and the striking sequence were so convincingly correct that it is difficult to imagine how the fly could have been dislodged, but it was. In the offshore game even when you do things right, you can still come up empty handed. Marlin one, Nick nothing.

Mike shook his head in disgust and I wished him better luck when he took his turn. We didn't voice it at the time but neither one of us had high hopes that he would get a chance to cast to a marlin. Time was running short and the skipper had altered the trolling pattern that put us on a course for home. I don't know for how long, but both of us dosed off and were suddenly jolted back to reality when the skipper yelled, "*Viene, viene,*" (he's coming, he's coming). I didn't need to revert to my high

False albacore are built for high-speed, line-burning sprints.

school Spanish to understand that a marlin had homed in on a teaser and was fast approaching the boat looking for more. The mate cleared the boat line, Mike reeled in the second teaser and I had the third line with a marlin trying to rip the strip bait from my hands. The marlin had the lure in its grasp and shook its head like a dog playing with a rag doll. When I finally wrenched it from its jaws it was like taking an ice cream cone from a greedy kid. But Mike was quick to provide instant appeasement and the marlin took the fly with the kind of attitude that read, "This is mine, and you're not going to get it back." In fact, Mike didn't get it back. Despite all his experience, he was awe-struck by the fish's aerial acrobatics behind the boat. This is the kind of excitement you have to experience first hand to realize the magnitude of the mesmerizing effect it has one's reactions. The fact that the fly was still firmly planted after the first few seconds of violent head shakes and

snake-like body contortions confirmed that the hook had thoroughly penetrated the fish's jaw.

However, a positive hook set is only one phase in a series of requirements that must be met to ensure that the contest ends in the angler's favor. Most saltwater species go wild when they feel the hook and this is particularly the case with acrobatic fish like billfish, bluefish, dorado, makos and tarpon. After setting the hook, the first order of business is to gain control of any remaining line that is lying on deck or in a stripping basket. With any fast-moving species, and this can run the piscatorial alphabet from albacore to yellowfin, the line lying at your feet will streak upward like a snake on steroids. If there were an ideal situation for the application of Murphy's Law, this is certainly it. Line moving at this speed can foul on any number of protuberances including shoelaces, belt buckles, shirt cuffs, jewelry, eyeglasses, hat brims, rod butts, reel handles and perhaps most obvious of all, boat cleats. It was the latter that proved to be Mike's nemesis.

One proven method of clearing the outgoing line is to grasp it lightly between the thumb and index finger of the line hand. Hold the rod shoulder high with the butt end pressed against your forearm. Then rotate the rod so the reel handle faces away from the outgoing line. Watch the line, not the fish, to make sure it shoots cleanly through the guides. In the early years of this sport, some anglers were of the opinion that the best way to clear line was to form a ring with the thumb and forefinger to serve as a channel. This may help direct the line's path, but the fact that it is no longer in contact with your fingers, deprives you of full control, something you do not want to relinquish at this critical period. If you do, you're courting disaster.

Mike of course, is well versed in all this, but a wildly cavorting marlin putting on an aerial display a few scant yards from your rod tip is a very compelling sight. Only seconds elapsed, but when he took his eyes off the fish and looked down, a section of line had already wrapped around a stern cleat. The finality was like a constrictor coiling its prey. Mike frantically tried to clear it, but it was too late. The 20-pound-class tippet parted and marlin number two dished out another plate of humble pie. At least we had some cold cervezas left.

Having It Out With Your Quarry: Fish-Fighting Tactics

If there were such a thing as graduate schools for fish-fighting techniques, the supreme learning institutes would be on the decks of the San Diego-based long-range boats plying the waters south of the border. As a sequel to my first book on long-range fishing, *Hot Rail*, in 1990 I had a second work published entitled, *Doing it Standup Style*. I chose this title because I wanted to depict the unique character of this form of big-game fishing. When you fish standup style, you go one-on-one with your quarry without benefit of a fighting chair or the boat chasing the fish. To this day I stand by the claim I made back then—regardless of the tackle choice, this mode of angling ranks as one of the ultimate challenges in sport fishing. Forgive me if I remain somewhat unimpressed by the gargantuan catches recorded by some bluewater buffs who are strapped in a chair while the boat roars full blast in reverse as it backs down on the fish. I have friends who've managed to capture the elusive "grander" and they're justly proud of their accomplishments. I also realize that there is no way you could realistically battle a critter this size standing up with a hand-held rod. Nonetheless, in terms of physical stamina and fish-fighting skill, trying to subdue a brute standup style that may weigh 75% less than the 1000-pounder is a much more difficult task.

In all the years I've been on these boats, I've seen an incredible array of fish-fighting outcomes. On the tragic end of the scale, I saw a guy hit the deck from a massive heart attack while he was locked on to a giant yellowfin. Things like this can happen in a tranquil trout stream, but I'm convinced that the big tuna did this guy in. On the brighter side, I saw a young man confined to a wheelchair land a 200-pound-class tuna, a feat that made even hardened deck hands dry their eyes a few times. I've also witnessed what seem like apparent contradictions. There have been instances where medium-size yellowfin in the 50- to 70-pound-class took twice as long to land as their bigger and supposedly stronger brothers topping the 100-pound mark. But more to the topic at hand, I've been there when he-man lumberjacks and firefighters found themselves pinned to the rail, while two rather petite female anglers pulling on the same class of fish brought their tuna to gaff with

Captain Bill Matthews cradling his client's Pacific bonito taken at Catalina Island.

little more than a healthy dose of perspiration. I can only speculate regarding the former occurrences, but the latter instances where the ladies outperformed their stronger male counterparts, has a simple explanation. They knew how to fight fish. They had what we call technique. The macho boys did not.

In standup-style fishing, if you lack technique, you pay the price because the fish, particularly the tunas, will definitely put the hurt on you. Being pinned to the rail is a very uncomfortable position. There are a number of colorful expressions like, "praying to the tuna gods," or "making love to the teak," that depict these unfortunate set of circumstances, but they're only funny if you're not the one on the other end of the line. I can recall numerous instances where the deckhands would be thoroughly wiped out only halfway through a trip because they were constantly being asked to take over the fish-fighting chores for anglers who had to literally throw in the towel. I have vivid memories of one fellow who took the dykes from his belt and cut his line. Before any of us could ask for an explanation, he looked at the skipper and said, "I didn't pay all this money to get in a position like this."

The big-game, 14- and 16-weight fly outfits may be far less heavy and cumbersome than comparable conventional tackle rigs, but the demands placed on angler and equipment from strong-pulling fish can be every bit as taxing. In many respects however, the fish-fighting principles are the same and if you want to do both yourself and the fish justice, develop good technique. Of course, even then there is no assurance that you'll win the contest.

Two of the most epic battles I've ever been engaged in with fly gear occurred when Bill Barnes and I were fishing together. The first encounter took place in the mid-1980s at his lodge, Casa Mar. It was the latter part of May. Bill used to close camp for the summer months back then and I was anxious to spend the last week of the season with him. It turned out to be some of the best fishing I'd ever experienced. As Lefty would put it, "It was so good, you thought it was yesterday." The water was unusually calm and there were acres of tarpon a few hundred yards outside the river mouth. For three consecutive days I fought tarpon all day long. I would skip the delicious lunches because I had to spend the time replenishing my supply of flies and leaders. I already had years of experience down here and when I packed for the trip, I was confident that I had enough to see me through the week. But the tarpon fishing had never been so furious and the silver kings were taking a toll.

The last of the remaining guests reluctantly left after the third day and Bill and I finally got our chance to fish together. Just by virtue of where he lives, "Señor Beel" as his staff likes to call him, has taken more than a lifetime's share of tarpon. After what I believe was the fourth fish that morning, he suggested we try something different and run outside the river mouth a few miles. I was not happy with his proposal and good friends that we are, I let him know it. My protests notwithstanding, it was his boat, and his lodge, so his desire to explore won out over my rekindled love affair with tarpon. We

didn't run more than a mile when we both spotted a lone frigate bird methodically circling an area like a buzzard hovering over carrion. We headed in its direction but did not have expectations of anything significant because the water was still clouded from the jungle silt pouring out of the river. With the bow rope in my hands for added support, I stood on the johnboat's casting platform for a better viewing position. At about 200 yards where the bird was circling, I saw a surface break. Bill saw it too and revved the outboard to give us a little more speed. Closing the distance, we could see that the surface was in turmoil from breaking fish. At first we were not sure what they were but as we slid into the melee, we could see yellowfin tuna jumping clear out of the water. Bill immediately had to reaffirm what a good idea he had and naturally I provided enthusiastic support for his decision.

We had four outfits onboard, three 12-weight fly rigs we used for tarpon and one 15-pound plug-casting combination that Bill liked for snook. He picked up the plug outfit and fired out a red-and-white 35M Mirrorlure. He only managed about two complete turns on the reel handle when he yelled, "I'm on." The little Shimano bait-casting reel held only about 150 yards of line and this was all taken in seconds. Bill looked at the empty spool and said, "That was quick." I grabbed my fly rod, quickly stripped some line off the reel, worked the head outside the rod tip and made a cast. I, too, was on seconds after the fly landed on the water. In this case however, both of us saw the tuna eat the fly about 15 feet from the boat. Here we go again, trying to guess a fish's size. In the brief moment we saw the yellowfin, we figured it to be close to the 100-pound mark. Bill laughed when the tuna took off and said, "This isn't going to take long." At the rate line was disappearing from the Tarpon model Billy Pate reel, I had to agree.

This is phase-one of the contest with tuna and part of a reaction pattern manifested by a variety of game fish when they realize they are hooked. The initial run is pure, unadulterated excitement and there is little more you can do at this point other than hang on, relish the experience and hope the fish doesn't take all the line. One advantage of fishing the open ocean is that you seldom have to worry about the fish getting into structure where they can foul the line or cut you off. But in addition to getting spooled, in this type of fishing you have other things to worry about. The hook could pull loose, the increased drag from all the line in the water could overtax the tippet's breaking strength or a shark might intercept your quarry. If you spend any time on the offshore grounds, inevitably you can expect to suffer all these mishaps.

Miraculously, I survived the first phase. I could see patches of the gold spool through the few remaining wraps of backing. We didn't have a meter on the boat, so I have no idea what the depth was, but my guess is the yellowfin ended its downward descent simply because it ran out of water. Now I was in the second phase of the battle. The fish has settled in the depths and I was faced with the back-breaking task of muscling it back to the surface. It's in phase one when you hear all the whoops and hollers because it's such an exhilarating sensation to feel that initial surge of raw power as the fish tears away with your fly. Whether it's a bluefin or a bonefish, the thrill coefficient will tweak all your senses. It's different in phase two. Now you have to go to work. Just like humans, there is infinite variation in how fish react in their effort to survive, but despite the idiosyncrasies unique to each encounter, there are basic fighting principles that have uniform application.

If you want to land big fish on light tackle, you will have to learn to apply maximum pressure on your quarry. Two of the very best at this game are Stu Apte and the late Harry Kime. Stu will tell you that the opposing force must be smooth, and it must be relentless. If you or your drag jerks, very likely the class tippet will break. If the pressure isn't constant, the struggle is needlessly prolonged. As Harry was fond of saying, "When you rest, the fish rests." It's amazing how sound advice has a way of jogging your memory precisely at the time you need it most. Here I am in a 16-foot johnboat, tussling with a tuna that is dogging me so hard I cannot lift the tip of my 12-weight Fenwick Fenglass rod out of the water. I knew that Harry had been in situations like this before when he fished yellowfin in Baja and Bill reminded me of what he must have felt like. But I also reminded myself of what Harry drilled into me many years before when I first started to tackle bluewater species on fly gear.

The situation may seem like a standoff, but you cannot expect to move the fish by simply maintaining a bend in the rod. The rod is a lever and you have to work it like one. If you are not gaining any line with the rod in one position, change the angle of pressure by moving the rod from one side to the other and keep the angle as low as possible. As Stu has demonstrated innumerable times, you cannot exert as much pressure when the rod has a steep, vertical bend in it. You can prove this to yourself by grasping the tag end of approximately 20 feet of line while another person holding the rod

changes fighting angles. You will feel the most resistance when the other person pulls back with the rod positioned at about 45 degrees. I also made sure that my hands stayed locked on the rod grip. If you slide your hand up the rod shaft, you may experience temporary relief from the strain on your wrist and arm, but this is not a good move. High sticking in hockey is a penalty. When fighting fish it can be a disaster. Sliding your hand forward of the rod grip changes the fulcrum point. The primary lifting power of the rod is in the butt section and you eliminate a significant portion of this when you pull on the rod above the grip. You also increase the chances of shattering the rod.

I had plenty of time to think about all this as minutes began to run into hours. Just for my own interest I like to know how much time elapses when I'm fighting a big fish and periodically I would ask Bill to check his watch. I couldn't believe it when he told me an hour and 45 minutes had ticked by and I still didn't have much to show for my efforts. Bill guessed that we probably drifted about 2 1/2 miles, a good indication that the tuna was actually towing us. Our fuel was running low and to save as much as possible for the ride back to the lodge, we decided that I would fight the fish from a dead boat. As far as tiring the fish is concerned, this can be a double-edged sword. On the plus side is the fact that there is less likelihood of popping the tippet because of the rubber band-like effect of pulling from a small, free-drifting boat. The boat simply slid in the direction from which I was pulling. This brought to mind a story Harry told me years ago about one of his exploits in Baja when he was fishing from a float tube, something I definitely do not recommend. He was about 50 yards off the beach when he hooked a nice-size yellowtail. Yellows are close cousins to amber jack and are noted for their incredible pulling power. During the initial stages of the encounter Harry was enjoying the duel, but after about 15 minutes, when he noticed the shoreline was almost a mile behind him, he started to become concerned. Thoughts about becoming part of the food chain began to occupy his mind and he felt uncomfortable about being so far from shore. Eventually, as he found himself being towed further and further offshore, he decided to break the fish off, but to his dismay, he found that the sling-shot effect of pulling from the float tube prevented him from doing so. He would pull back all he could to try and pop the 16-pound tippet but the float tube would shoot forward canceling his effort. He might as well have been pulling against a piling. Finally, in a desperate attempt to free himself from the fish, Harry took several wraps of line around the rod just below the reel and reared back as fast and sharp as he could. The tippet broke and Harry fought the effects of fatigue to kick his way back in as quickly as possible.

Harry's tale highlights the disadvantage of fighting a big fish from a small, unanchored boat. The platform you are standing on does not afford much in the way of resistance making it very difficult to effectively pressure the fish. This was the problem with which I was confronted. If the tuna managed much of an angle away from the boat, most of my pulling effort did little more than drag us along with the fish.

Finally, after about three hours when the yellowfin finally started sulking in the depths directly below the boat, I felt that my pulling efforts started to have some effect. The progress was agonizingly slow. I would

Kathy, the author's wife, enjoying the initial run of a striper on the flats.

manage maybe three-quarters of a turn on the direct-drive handle and retrieve a few inches of line. The tuna would react by taking back the little I had gained. This is characteristic of the give-and-take kind of struggle you experience with a game fish who senses it is in a battle for its life. For your part, you may be nearing physical exhaustion. Your hands may cramp, your arms feel like they have lead weights hanging from them and your legs are signaling that they can't continue the marathon. If all this sounds a little too dramatic, you haven't played

tug of war with a beer barrel-size tuna. For those of you who have, you know what I'm talking about. You have to ask yourself how bad you want to win the contest. If you're absolutely determined, you hang in there and continue to endure the punishment, which can be psychological as well as physical. It's very disheartening to have the fish run off with yards of line in a matter of seconds that may have taken you a half hour to earn, but that's how it is especially when you tangle with members of the tuna clan. Everyone in this family is in top physical condition. No heart trouble, no weak lungs, no deteriorating joints, just highly-toned muscle that keeps these metabolic dynamos in perpetual motion from birth to death. As I've said many times before, there is no such thing as an out-of-shape tuna.

Having fought tuna with all kinds of tackle, it's no exaggeration when I admit that these fish have exhausted me far more than any human adversary in a lifetime of contact sports. Three hours had elapsed and I only had about 25 yards of backing back on the spool. I had been this route before and it had the makings of another bitter defeat. But then as hour number four approached I started to retain the miserly lengths of line I cranked back on the spool.

The technique I used is called short-stroking and it was pioneered and developed on the West Coast long-range boats. Instead of trying to lift the rod to a nearly vertical position, the tip is raised only a foot or so above the horizontal plane. The tip is then quickly lowered while you simultaneously take a turn on the reel handle. When you do this in fairly rapid succession it helps keep the fish off balance. The effect is like barraging a boxer with a series of quick jabs. After a while this begins to take its toll. Secondly, and most importantly, the short lifting stroke prevents the fish from making a head-long dive. If you raise the rod real high, the resulting long down stroke gives the fish a chance to get its head down and where the head goes, the body follows. This, of course, is what you are trying to avoid because the fish is going to continue to take line. Back in my youth on the jackpole fleet, I was constantly drilled about the importance of not allowing the fish to get its head down. With a rod-and-reel combination, at least the fish can take line. But when there is no reel, something has to give. The pole may break, the fisherman could be pulled overboard or, in my case, the pole was wrenched from my bleeding hands. The four experienced salts fishing alongside me laughed like hell, but the tough old Sicilian captain told me in no uncertain terms that the pole, line and jig combination would be deducted from my pay and that if I wanted to stay on the boat, it better not happen again. It didn't.

Thoughts of the old boy came to mind as I started to gain on this fish. My fatigue registry was temporarily blunted as I imagined his reaction to this ordeal. He would be laughing and shouting obscenities (most of which I never understood) at this utterly fruitless enterprise. Wasting hours to land a fish that should have been bounced on deck in seconds was something he would never understand. Then add to that the fact that I shelled out a considerable sum of money to partake in such foolishness, and he would be convinced that I had totally lost it. Different strokes for different folks would not have set with him. The only stroke that interested him was the one that put the fish on the boat.

At least I was finally getting closer to that objective. After four and a half, grueling hours under a relentless tropical sun, for the first time in the contest, I began to feel confident that this time I would be the victor. The tuna began to make wide circles in the depths below, a clear sign that the fish is beginning to tire. Bill commented on that fact and I mumbled back that I was thoroughly beat. But I knew that this was a critical stage of the struggle. After such a prolonged period the hook can tear the fleshy part of the mouth and pull free. Big tuna have a good set of teeth that can wear through line, but with the 80-pound bite leader I was using, I felt I had that contingency covered. Sharks are another worry at this stage. They always seem to be in the area with tuna and the circling phase is where the fish is most vulnerable to attack. Their tail beats have slowed and sharks know they are in trouble. In a few cases I've seen anglers with heavy, standup conventional gear actually pull a tired but frantic tuna from pursuing sharks but it doesn't happen often. With fly rods the situation is totally hopeless. We didn't see any, but we knew the area

was shark infested with a large population of very aggressive bull sharks. These fearsome critters are close cousins of the great white and have a distinctly nasty disposition. I have seen them make short work of 100-pound tarpon, knocking them 10 feet in the air with bite marks that look like gouges in a topsoil mound worked over by a backhoe.

Famed Casa Mar guide, Suerdo, lip gaffs a tarpon prior to release.

Despite the agonizing protests from my body, I knew I had to keep pulling, but I also knew when to pull. As the fish makes it circle, the point at which you want to try and gain as much line as possible is when the tuna is turning toward the boat. The fish is already coming your way and you should take advantage of the situation by short-pumping as much line as possible. In contrast, attempting to pull when the fish is moving away from the boat can be the wrong move even when heavy tackle is employed. I was alongside a friend of mine who was desperately trying to land what would have been his first yellowfin over 200 pounds. We could clearly see the fish in the depths below and it looked as big as a living room couch. The tuna was in its circling phase and my friend thought he would finally break the fish's spirit if he could force it toward the boat while it was swimming away. This proved to be a miscalculation because the combination of the tuna's forward inertia coupled with the added resistance applied by the angler broke his 80-pound-test line. My yellowfin was half that size, but with a class tippet rated at 16-pound test, there was little room for error.

Ever so slowly I began gaining on the fish. The tuna's resistance was still formidable but it was clear that it was losing strength. Bill even began to question what we would do with the fish once I had it alongside the boat. He didn't have to worry. My 30-pound Dacron backing suddenly and unexpectedly parted. To this day I don't have an explanation. It was new line from a reputable manufacturer. If anything were to break, it should have been the weak link in the chain, the 16-pound-class tippet. To say I was dejected doesn't quite cover it. I was drenched in sweat, the Fenglass rod had a set in it like a hula-hoop, and that evening at dinner, I had difficulty using a knife and fork. Chalk another one up for the tuna.

My second memorable bluewater battle was also in Costa Rica but this time it was on the Pacific side. Bill Barnes and I had been sail-fishing out of Bahia Pez Vela back in June of 1984 and the action was nothing short of spectacular. One day Bill and I raised 64 sailfish, Billy Pate broke the existing 8-pound-tippet record with a 78-pound Pacific sail and Jack Samson established a roosterfish record with a 31-pound, 12-ounce specimen he nailed on a popper.

On the last day of our two-week stay, the action slowed to the point where several hours would pass without raising a single fish. It's easy to lose concentration at times like this and we both dozed off confident that the skipper and mate would promptly alert us if something popped up behind one of the teasers. It was just a few minutes past noon when the captain yelled, "*Vela, vela, vela, grande.*" That meant sailfish and a big one at that. We could see the huge dorsal fin behind the starboard teaser and like a well-honed team we quickly attended to our pre-assigned tasks. The past week had afforded us plenty of practice. I cleared the teaser on the port side and got ready with my fly rod. Ten days fishing took two of my 12-weight rods out of commission. These were high-quality sticks, but fly-rod technology was not what it is today and both rods broke at the ferrule when I was trying to pump fish from the depths. Bill suffered his own share of mishaps. One of his rods shattered and the cork handle on another worked loose. For this last days' fishing I rigged a rod that Jack Erskine had built for me in Australia. I never learned who the blank manufacturer was, but this is one great rod and I was fortunate to be fishing it that day. I combined it with the same reel I used throughout the trip, my direct-drive, Billy Pate Marlin. This also was an ideal choice.

Bill had the fish on the strip-bait teaser and shouted something to the effect that this was the largest sailfish he had ever seen. On closer inspection it became apparent that the crazed critter mauling the teaser was a blue marlin. Bill had to wrench the dorado belly strip bait away from the marlin on five separate occasions before he finally managed to clear it from the water so I could make the cast. The fish was so enraged that it would charge the transom and dart in and out looking for the meal that continually evaded him. On the fifth try, the captain was able to get the boat far enough forward to put it in neutral so I could cast to the fish. I will never forget the moment it took the fly. The head came out of the water and the bill slashed from side to side like a swordsman trying to flail away at the devil. With all the thrashing on the surface, I never actually saw the take. My feather duster-size blue-and-white streamer was no longer in sight and Bill confirmed the obvious when he shouted, "He's got it, he's got it." I waited those precious few seconds for the line to come tight in my hands and then struck back with a succession of three quick jabs. Now for the first time, I could actually see the streamer pinned back in its mouth in the upper corner of the jaw. I was glad it was there, but silhouetted against the marlin's natural beauty, it looked like a gaudy decoration that simply didn't belong.

The fish never jumped. Instead, it sped out away from the boat peeling line from the reel like it was being stripped by one of those high-speed winding machines used in tackle shops. Even with the enormous line capacity of the Marlin model reel, I would have been spooled in short order if the boat hadn't followed the fish. A few times we actually got alongside the blue and could get a clear view of its awesome size. Our boat was a 26-foot pocket cruiser and the marlin from the tip of its bill to its tail was easily half its length. The only confirmation I have of this is about 15 seconds of shaky video that Bill shot from the bridge. The captain estimated the blue to be somewhere between 350 and 400 pounds. Naturally, this didn't encourage me.

Those few times the captain maneuvered the boat alongside the fish, we could have taken it with a flying gaff. But what would that have proven? We would have killed the fish, but legitimately I could never have gone on record as having actually beat the fish. For IGFA record purposes, Bill, the captain, or the mate could have attempted a shot with a hand-held gaff, but they all knew it would have been a fruitless, as well as potentially dangerous, move. The marlin was still "green," which means that it was nowhere near ready to be stuck with a hand gaff. Bill had years of experience as a mate on South Florida charter boats and he knew full well the dangers of planting a gaff in a fish that still had plenty of life in it. I saw my friend Jerry Pierce get two of his ribs broken when he gaffed a striped marlin that wasn't quite ready to give up the fight. He leaned over, stuck the fish in its side and proceeded to have his chest bashed against the rail as the marlin thrashed the surface. In my case, a flying gaff where the head detaches and is roped off to a boat cleat would more than likely have done its job and I would have had the first blue marlin ever taken on regulation fly gear. But as far as fly-rod records are concerned, a flying gaff disqualifies a catch and I for one hope the regulation remains in force. I know there are those who disagree, but I feel that you either land the fish in the conventional manner or you don't.

It had been five hours since I hooked the fish and judging by it tremendous reserves of power, I had done little to tire it. I would gain a few turns of line, only to have the blue react by taking back much more. The captain had to have the boat in gear the entire time, constantly tracking the fish. We were going further and further out to sea, fuel was getting low, there was no radar aboard and the weather began to look ominous. For the better part of five hours I had what could best be described as a tenuous connection with one of the most magnificent creatures that swims the seas. I probably didn't inconvenience it all that much because it continued to swim at will. Bill remarked that maybe it was feeding or looking for a mate. We'll never know because I had to sever the connection. If my safety were the only thing at stake, I would have stayed out for as long as it would take to reach some final culmination of the contest, but I wasn't alone and the time had come to head back in. I clamped down on the spool, pointed the rod directly at the fish and broke it off. Not to wax philosophical, but I guess it wasn't meant to be.

A low-angle pulling force applied from side to side is effective not only for big-game, bluewater species. It should be applied in all fish-fighting encounters. A Christmas Island coral head about the size of a gymnasium floor was the battleground where this technique was convincingly demonstrated to three trout fishermen from Chicago. They were fishing this spot with two other Florida-based anglers who managed to land five, 15-pound-class trevally between them. The Chicago trio was having a terrible time. One guy had his only weight-forward floating fly line cut almost in half so he had to stop fishing. The other two were hooking fish, but they never landed any.

Compared to the fellows from Florida, it was obvious that the trio did not have good fish-fighting technique.

Every fish they hooked managed to make it to the end of the coral head where they dove for deeper water. In the process of doing so, the line made contact with the scalpel-sharp coral and the fish immediately gained its freedom. None of them put any significant pressure on the fish. They just stood there with the rod held high while the fish scorched across the flat.

After losing his third trevally, I told the disgusted angler to watch one of the Florida fellows who was on to another fish. Like his partner, this young fellow never allowed the fish to sprint the 80 or so yards to the end of the coral head. He kept the rod low and applied pressure from the side. When the fish began to turn in that direction, he would flip the rod over to the opposite side and apply pressure from this new direction. Each time the fish turned, the angler pulled from the opposite side. This is a tactic that can wear a fish down in short order. Not only does the constant change of direction keep the fish off balance, it also robs it of its ability to resist to the utmost because it's forced to swim away with a line that is low and to the side of its dorsal area. To give you some idea of the effect this has on the fish's pulling power, envision a situation where you had to pull a concrete block walking forward with a rope. The most efficient way to do this would be to throw the rope over your shoulder. This is what you allow the fish to do when the rod is held high with the line directly over the center plane of its dorsal fin. In contrast, with the rod pointed low and to the side of the fish, the effect is like trying to pull the block with your arms and hands to one side of your body, a difficult maneuver.

The young man from Florida was the epitome of a southern gentleman. After landing his fish, he went over to the guy with the cut-up fly line and handed him his outfit. In about 10 minutes time he hooked another trevally and we coached him through the fish-fighting process. The guy was amazed at how much pressure you can exert with a 9-weight rod and a 12-pound-test tippet. Although it felt awkward at first, he maintained a low fighting angle and constantly altered the direction of side pressure. Gradually he got the feel of things and we didn't have to tell him when or how to pull. Experience is a great teacher and Christmas Island makes for a wonderful classroom setting. The guy landed his first trevally and that night he treated us to a round of drinks at dinner. His buddies were all enthusiastic pupils and by the end of the week, their fighting techniques improved dramatically. As we parted company at the airport, one of them shouted that Midwest trout streams would never be the same.

Reading the Water

Of course, to experience the thrill of trying to subdue fish on fly gear, you first have to locate them. A guide or some other experienced angler can be invaluable when you're in unfamiliar waters, saving you time and often sparing you considerable frustration. If you choose to go it alone and are not content to leave this simply to chance, you will have to learn to read the water. There are no man-made fish locators posted on the water, but there are signs and if you learn to interpret them, they are as useful in finding fish as a nautical chart is for navigation.

The most dramatic sign of all, is when you can actually see the fish. It doesn't even have to be the entire body. A tail or dorsal fin sticking out of the water is one of the most stimulating sights an angler can witness and is one of the principal attractions of fishing shallow

When bait concentrate into tightly packed pods, predator game fish are usually not far behind.

water. Two summers ago my friend Jimmy Orfice took me over to Fisher's Island, a short distance from the Connecticut-Rhode Island shore. Like his dad, Jim is a first-rate angler and despite his years of experience in these waters, he loves to explore new spots. In the early afternoon with the sun high in the sky we sight-fished for stripers along the Island's beaches and had a great time spying bass over the sand flats and watching them disappear into patches of rocks and eelgrass.

But the most excitement came at dusk when Jim decided to explore a little cove that was glassed over like a Midwest farm pond. He shut the engine off and we both paddled the 13-foot Whaler through an opening between some boulders that put us in a salt pond about the size of a football field. At first, our only company was hordes of hungry mosquitoes that were tough to ward off even with the bug juice. We were just about to vacate the area when we both spotted a pair of dorsal fins only inches above the surface. Now we totally lost consciousness of the mosquitoes buzzing in our ears and chewing on exposed patches of skin. Jim's hunch that stripers might be in here to dine on the baitfish that had been washed in with the incoming tide was correct and the sight of them finning the placid surface was an added bonus. For some reason we were more excited seeing the fins barely break the surface than we were earlier in the day when we could spot the entire fish. Maybe it had something to do with the anticipation that there is more to come. I hooked and landed one bass that taped out at 30 inches, which lead us to speculate that even larger stripers might be in the spot. But after releasing the fish, we didn't see anymore fins and there were no more strikes. The struggling striper probably spooked everything that was in there, but the sight of those fins etching their way across the surface keeps calling us back to that spot.

The sight of protruding tails on a bonefish flat can also stir your sole. One of the largest concentrations I had ever seen was near a small island chain referred to as Tres Marias in Mexico's Ascension Bay. I thought the guide shared an object lesson in understatement when he told me he was taking me to a good spot. I got out of the skiff with him and we walked around the point of one of the islands where off in the distance he pointed to a large gray patch that was prominently highlighted against the surrounding tan bottom. As I got closer, it was difficult to control my excitement when I realized that they were tailing bonefish. There were so many tails and they were so closely clustered that from a distance you might possibly mistake it for some kind of partially exposed structure like a rock or coral bed. The giveaway of course, was the fact that there was periodic movement. Wavelets washing over rocks can give the illusion of movement, but at 50 yards there was no question that the patch before me was the real thing. Like hogs in a trough, the bonefish had their heads down greedily grubbing at what the nutrient-rich bottom had to offer. In seesaw fashion, the head goes down, and the tail goes up, just like your heart rate. The stimulation to your senses is all-consuming.

When a part of the fish is exposed, the reflection from the sun can be the sign that first catches your eye. With bonefish it's usually the glint from the flat side of the tail fin. In the case of larger species like tarpon, the telltale sign can be the flash from the silver-sided flanks. This was my favorite sight at Bill's lodge, Casa Mar. Probably for most anglers who have fished the area, the biggest turn-on would be the sight of acres of tarpon busting the surface just outside the river mouth. It's an incredible scene to witness, but as much as I love being in the midst of such action, for me, the distant sight of shinning silver slashes flashing on the mirror-smooth surface of Simi Lagoon was the supreme visual experience. Just motoring along the serpentine tributaries flanked by the dense growth of the rain forest is an awesome experience in its own right and with all the sights and sounds flooding your senses, it's easy to lose track of the fact that you came here to fish. Inevitably it was the gradual slowing of the outboard as the guide prepared to enter the lagoon that caused me to refocus my thoughts on the encounters that lie ahead. My guide Seurdo, who was always fond of confirming the obvious, would say, "Get ready man, dey here."

In terms of sensory input, actually sighting fish is the most stimulating, but the sensation of sound has its own special drama, particularly when vision is restricted as is often the case with fog or at night. Stu Apte and I shared an unforgettable experience on a long-range fly-fishing trip we made together. It was our turn to take the option of fishing off the main vessel (the *Royal Star*) on one of the inflatables. Despite the limited visibility, we welcomed the chance to get off by ourselves with the deckhand. Fog can develop very rapidly over the ocean

CAPTAIN JOE BLADOS

and in a matter of minutes we were completely enveloped in a soup-like mist. The inflatable was only 14 feet long and Stu and I had difficulty seeing one another. We weren't too concerned because we were only about 50 yards from the *Royal Star*, we had radio communication and we were drifting together in the same direction. For safety's sake however, we decided to hold off casting until the fog lifted. In the distance we could hear the steady drone of the *Star's* generators, which given the circumstances, provided an extra measure of security. Suddenly the engine sounds were eclipsed by a thunderous, thrashing noise on the surface. For an instant the three of us were startled but this reaction quickly changed to one of excited anticipation once we realized there were fish breaking all around us. The sound reminded me of the prop wash noise I used to hear as a kid hanging around the tugboats in New York harbor. Stu, always the gentleman, insisted that I make a cast into the thrashing froth and I was on instantly. Our suspicions that it was probably yellowfin that were causing all the commotion were verified about 40 minutes later when I had a fat, football-shaped specimen alongside the boat that we guessed was about 35 pounds. By this time the fog had lifted and we could see bent rods all along the rail of the *Royal Star.*

John Posh, who prowls the Connecticut coastline at night with the stealth of a Navy Seal, taught me the importance of being alert for the sounds of fish on the feed in the dark. On one of my first night forays with him back in the early 70s we were wading a stretch of beach not far from his home in Stratford. I was having a difficult time picking my way through the rock-strewn shoreline and started complaining to him that there must be other places to wade that didn't feel like you were walking over greased bowling balls. He started to laugh and then abruptly told me to be quiet. Somewhat irritated, I answered back, "Big deal the fish can't hear us." John's immediate reply was, "Yeah, but I can't hear the fish." At first I thought he was kidding, but by the tone of his voice the second time he told me to shut my mouth and open my ears, I realized he was serious. After a half minute or so, he quietly asked, "Did you hear that?" I felt kind of stupid, but I didn't hear anything unusual and he told me to keep listening. A few more seconds went by and then I heard a succession of popping sounds coming from the inky blackness in front of us. John whispered, "They're bass and they've moved in closer. Put a slider on and work it slow, I think they're taking stuff on top." By this time I wasn't about to question his words of wisdom. I tied the slider on and a 27-inch striper exploded on it the first cast. Day or night, surface strikes really jolt your senses. John hooked up soon afterward and then I heard him curse. Bluefish must have been mixed in with the bass and he was cut off almost as soon as he set the hook. He tied on his last slider and connected with a bass almost identical to mine. The action didn't last long, but if it wasn't for John's sharp ears, I would have probably by passed the area and missed out on the fish that were there. Now whenever I'm night fishing, I make it a point to listen for possible signs of fish.

Years later fishing Lobsterville Beach with Popovics, Ed Jaworoski, and Lance Erwin, our less than subdued chatter was suddenly interrupted by very audible popping sounds that seemed to be only a few yards in front of where we were walking. The action had been very slow most of the evening and we all decided to make the long trek to Dogfish Bar where we hoped we would find bass. Trudging through the sand in chest-high waders can be pretty taxing even when you're fresh, but we were all tired from chasing bluefish on the beach earlier that afternoon. Nevertheless, this is what you can expect to endure if you spend much time working the shore and we stoically accepted the walk as part of paying the price to get into fish. Happily fate was with us that night because we didn't have to walk very far. Lance was in front of the pack and he was the first to hear what he thought were breaking fish. When he stopped, no one had to tell us to cut the chatter. We all stood silently straining to hear whatever the water was trying to tell us. It didn't take long for the sounds to register. Stripers were feeding right in front of us and we had the spot all to ourselves. We were into bass for about a half hour when the familiar popping tune of feeding fish was supplanted with wilder thrashing sounds on the surface. Ed, in a voice that clearly registered some concern, shouted, "Guys that doesn't sound like bass to me." Then Lance added, "It sounds like something is feeding on the bass." I was thinking the same thing when I asked Bob, who was fishing a few yards down to my right, to violate protocol and shine his high-beam flashlight into the water. Normally a light like this would put off fish and you will draw the wrath of fellow anglers if you start illuminating the area in front of you. Most experienced beach fishermen use low-intensity flashlights and some go so far as to turn around and face the beach whenever they have to shine it. This time however, it was just us guys, we had all caught fish, but more importantly, we were anxious to try and see what was out there causing all the commotion. Bob started fanning the area with his light when the beam flashed an object protruding from the surface. He had it concentrated in the light for a second and then it was gone. He started searching the area in front of him again when the beam caught the object a second time. "This thing is moving," he said. He lost sight of it again but quickly caught the direction of travel and was able to train the beam on it. "You guys won't believe this." I was in no mood for guessing games and before Bob could continue, I shouted, "You won't believe what? What the hell is it?" "It's a shark." Bob's simple reply rang in our ears like a fire alarm. We were little more than knee deep in the water, but every-one quickly backed up for the safety of the shoreline. Ed was the first one up on the beach loudly proclaiming that he didn't want to become part of the food chain. We couldn't determine what species of shark it was, or if there were more than one. In any case, it's one sound that won't be music to your ears if you're wading the water at night.

Aside from hearing acuity, relying on sound to alert you to the fact that fish are close at hand involves a good measure of plain old luck. However, luck is very fickle and if you simply leave things to chance, more often than not you'll come up short. If you want to get into fish with some measure of consistency, you will have to learn to read the signs that nature provides. But even when you find fish, if there aren't enough food sources, they will move on and you'll have to resort to the hunter mode once again.

On the long-range trip that Stu and I made together, we had both concerns well in hand. We relied on the skipper to put us in an area that held fish so it was no mere coincidence that we heard tuna breaking around the boat. Like any experienced guide, the skippers who ply these waters on a regular basis are extremely well versed in their craft and have an excellent record of consistently putting their passengers into fish. If they weren't, they would be out of business in short order. News travels fast in these fishing circles and captains who don't cut it soon find themselves looking for other kinds of work.

Once the fish are located, the ideal situation is one where you can hold them within casting range for as long as possible. This is where chum comes into play, something you normally don't have when fishing afoot, but it's a commodity the long-range boats carry in abundance. Stu and I didn't have to carry any on the inflatable because we were close enough to the mother ship to take advantage of the anchovies that were being tossed out to attract the tuna. Generally, with fast-moving species like members of the tuna family, if there isn't a sufficient quantity of chum on hand, the game becomes one of constant pursuit. The fish move into an area, decimate the bait population, then quickly move on to find new sources of nourishment.

Small-boat anglers whose chum supply may be limited or nonexistent and who fish for species like bluefish, bonito and false albacore know this chase scene well. You have to be prepared to move quickly, but before hitting the throttles, you also must know what to look for. The sight of breaking fish on the horizon is always an exciting affair, but many times before the fish ever show themselves, the first sign to watch for is bird activity. "BB, BB," is what an old, Portuguese fisherman in the

jackpole fleet used to tell me. It meant birds and bait. Even with the advent of electronic locators that began to make their way into the fleet back then, the old-timers always made you post a lookout for bird activity. If you weren't accustomed to it, just a few hours in the crow's nest scanning the horizon with high-powered binoculars could give you raging headaches. Nevertheless, this was considered an important part of the daily routine on those boats back then and everyone pulled a shift in the nest. In that respect at least, things haven't changed much today. Whether it's commercial or recreational, if you're serious about saltwater fishing you learn to become a bird watcher.

Two of the best at this in the areas they normally fish are Scott Paciello and Captain Joe Mattioli. I like to think of them as the "Bird Men of Staten Island" because they've developed this into a fine art. Joe has the full complement of electronic fishing aids on his beautifully equipped Mako 22, but he and Scott love to fish by the birds. After fishing with them a few days last August, I can see why they're "birds of a feather." Almost as soon as we cleared the harbor, Joe made sure that we all "had our eyes on" because he wanted to make sure we didn't miss any aerial activity. Between the three of us I don't think there was anything that flew that day that escaped our attention, including the air traffic at JFK. Relentless though it was, the surveillance paid off. Joe was the first to point to diving birds at a lighthouse not far from the harbor. We motored over, he cut the engine to set us in a drift pattern, and we were promptly in to school size stripers. Next, we made our way over to Rockaway Point where all three of us spotted birds working the edge of the rip. Again we were into bass, but these were a little larger, measuring 25 to 32 inches in length. Scott spiced up the action with an "alligator blue" that hit the hand scale at 15 pounds. An hour and a half later we saw flocks of terns dive-bombing the surface with the Verrazano bridge and New York skyline as a backdrop. In all my years as a New Yorker, I've seen many shots of the waterfront, but I had never witnessed anything like this. I was thinking that if any of the commuters on the Verrazano bridge were fishermen who could see what was going on below, there would be a record-breaking chain car collision.

From a distance it can be difficult to determine whether surface breaks are caused by birds hitting the water or fish busting bait on top, but as we got closer it was clear that there were fish under the marauding flocks of birds. We didn't know what they were but judging by the boils, we could tell that they weren't very big. Scott got the first cast off with a small size Surf Candy and was struck instantly. His loose line shot up from deck like it was being propelled by a compressed-air canister, which prompted him to shout, "These things may be small but they can sure burn some line." Joe immediately quipped, "I'll bet it's false albacore," and indeed it was. We were in them for the better part of two hours. If we hadn't spotted the birds off in the distance, we would have missed out on all this action.

John Timmerman and a "Fat Albert" that
fell for his fly at Harker's Island.

Similar to the fish below, sea birds like gulls, terns, pelicans and frigates are constantly in search of food sources. The difference of course, is that we seldom see the fish, but the birds are almost always plainly visible. However, interpreting bird activity is not always so obvious. Terns for example, may be constantly swooping down on the surface picking up baitfish, but that doesn't necessarily indicate that larger predator fish are in the area. Birds feasting on small baitfish is a common sight on many of the tidal rips in the Northeast, but it is the particular pattern of bird activity that will signal whether or not those bait are being pursued by various game fish. Joe Blados was careful to point this out to my wife, Kathy who would get excited every time she saw birds working the surface. This was her first saltwater trip and on two successive occasions when Joe pulled up to diving birds, we were into a school of blues and she

hooked fish. After that, the first time Joe ran by a group of birds she didn't say anything, but she gave me a funny look. The second time he did this, she asked him why. He circled around and told her to study the way the birds were flying. With no prior experience in any of this, she wasn't able to discern anything of particular significance. "They're flying around, dipping down and eating all those poor little fish." "That's right," Joe said, "But notice the way they're flying. They're spread out, they're not packed in tight like they were when you hooked fish." That was the critical difference. The birds will tend to fly and feed in close formation when the baitfish are herded into tight packs by pursuing game fish. Conversely, when the bait are scattered, the birds roam the sky above looking to intercept a meal wherever they can. Of course, it's always wise to pay close attention anytime you see birds working the surface, but it's also true that a lot of time is wasted by inexperienced anglers who stop to investigate every instance of bird activity.

Another common mistake is to overlook the activity of a single bird or two. Too many anglers only pay attention if there are large numbers of birds working over an area, but many times a lone bird can be the signal for some very hot action. Recall the instance a few pages back where Bill Barnes and I found a large school of yellowfin tuna just by watching the flying pattern of a single frigate bird. A small patch of water with a lone bird flying overhead like it was assigned guard duty is worth exploring. That bird could be over bait that has drawn the attention of game fish. The area may seem devoid of life, but that could be the proverbial calm before the storm because action could erupt at any moment. I've seen this happen with yellowfin, striped marlin and yellowtail. Particularly in the case with striped marlin in Southern California and Mexico, a lone frigate bird will often hover overhead apparently waiting for the billfish to intercept a school of bait which makes easy pickings for the predator above.

Fishing from a panga off Cabo San Lucas with a local Mexican fisherman as a guide, I learned the importance of eyeballing lone frigate birds. In two weeks of fishing, these birds put us on marlin and yellowfin. If I were alone, I wouldn't have bothered to stop at the sight of a solo bird circling above, but I know better now and it paid big dividends with a bonanza yellowtail bite about 25 miles off the coast of Ensenada, Mexico.

Ensenada used to be known as the yellowtail capital of the world and there were a number of my high school days where the only school I attended consisted of hordes of yellows breezing off the Baja coast. It's sad to report that the fishery is a mere shadow of what it was years ago, but the last few seasons have seen something of a comeback. A friend and I launched his 20-foot, center console SeaCraft at Ensenada where we hoped to get into bluefin tuna that were reported to be in the area. A 20-footer may look big in a garage but when you're many miles off the coast, it's small. Nevertheless, I have confidence in the boat and my friend's seamanship abilities. The skiff has good range but lacking any sort of tower, visibility is limited. This wasn't too much of a handicap as far as spotting birds was concerned, but it did limit our ability to pick out floating patches of kelp that hugged the surface like a carpet. Kelp paddies and yellowtail go together like teenagers and fast cars. Baitfish are attracted to the apparent security of the floating kelp which in turn, attracts predators like yellowtail. The difficulty of course, is that you cannot expect to find fish under every kelp patch and where there are many floating in a given area, it's too time-consuming to try and check them all out. This is where birds can be a tremendous help. There may be only one or two over a single paddy, but if they are hanging over a particular patch, that is the one you definitely want to investigate.

From the boat's relatively low profile in the water, at first all we saw were two sea gulls methodically circling an area about 300 yards off our bow. It wasn't until we closed to almost half that distance that we could see they were hovering over a kelp paddy about the size of a double-bed mattress. We had already stopped on three previous paddies and found "no one home" at any of the patches. This one was different. It was occupied by a large school of yellowtail that were breezing around its perimeter. Every time they tore into the bait that was trying to take cover below the tangled kelp fronds, the gulls quickly swooped down and picked off the stunned and wounded. This was an ideal opportunity to start presenting flies because we were the only boat in the area. So many times a situation like is ruined because too many boaters do not know how to approach this type of structure. They will come roaring in and then at the last minute throttle down the engines. All this does is scare everything off. Instead, you should reduce engine speed to a point where the boat barely makes headway, *well* in advance of closing in on the paddy. You want to time this

so that you are about 50 yards or so out from the kelp. My friend Jim had been this route many times before and had the foresight to set up our drift pattern so that the wind was at our back. Obviously this made casting the flies a lot easier, but no less important, it gave the fly time to sink. If the boat were drifting away from the paddy, the fly line would be dragged along and the fly would never have a chance to sink more than a few feet below the surface. Unless you are casting poppers, the object here is to get the fly down because that is where

A Baja rooster near the end of its struggle.

the bait is. Occasionally you can draw some ferocious strikes on top, but the most consistent action is usually subsurface with streamers.

Because Jim was running the boat, I got off the first cast and let the line sink to a mental count of 20 before I started a medium-paced, hand-over-hand retrieve. These yellows were in the 15- to 20-pound-class range and even with the heavier 12- and 13-weight outfits we had rigged for bluefin, we weren't overgunned. When it comes to all-out pulling power, yellowtail can run with the best of them and there are few fish that can use structure to their advantage like they can. This is what I like about fishing them at offshore kelp paddies. Except for the paddy itself, in open water you don't have any rocks or reefs to worry about, so there is little chance that they will cut you off. But they will try to tangle you in the paddy, so you have to be prepared to apply maximum pressure. With yellows in this weight class, I recommend at least an 11-weight outfit.

I was fishing a 12-weight, and when that first fish hit and streaked for the depths, I was wishing that I had a heavier rod. Jim saw me bent over and quickly swapped his 12-weight for a 13. It was a good choice. He hooked up after me, his yellow was larger (definitely in the mid-20s) and he had it alongside the boat ready to be released at least 5 minutes before I even had my 15-pounder to color. We landed seven tails from that paddy which still ranks as my best day ever with yellows on the fly. When the bite finally shut off and we pulled away from the paddy, Jim's comment was, "So much for the birds."

Aside from bird activity, color can also be an indication that bait are present. Two years ago fishing aboard the *Sea Lion II* off Montauk, her sharp-eyed skipper Jimmy noticed a distinct patch of dark-colored water about 50 yards off the port bow. He shouted down from the bridge, "I'm not sure exactly what kind, but that's definitely a ball of bait out there. Get ready, I'm going to swing around to bring you into position to cast." There were no birds working in the area and there were no surface disturbances, just a dark-colored band that contrasted sharply with the blue water. But as we were soon to discover, that school of bait innocently silhouetted on the undulating surface had drawn fish to the area. Jack, the mate, cast a shiny chrome spoon with a spinning outfit and was bent after only a couple of cranks on the reel handle. I followed him with a blue-and-white Deceiver pattern that is my old standby whenever I go offshore. It quickly found its mark and I had my first bluefin tuna on fly. At not more than 5 pounds, the fish was definitely in the juvenile category but I was very happy despite its pint-size dimensions. I have been in many situations a lot more dramatic than this, with birds diving and fish breaking and have nonetheless still come away empty handed. By comparison, this scene was about as serene as it can get and it would have been easy for an untrained eye to just drive right past it. It also helps if you're not color blind.

When fishing inshore, it's important to be able to interpret the influence of various coastal features such as the contour of a beach, rock outcroppings, reefs, sea grass beds, kelp beds, bottom composition and a host of manmade structure such as piers, jetties, breakwaters and channels. Add in tidal influences, and you can see that the picture can become very complex. That's why if you expect to be able to successfully fish certain areas, you will have to learn to factor in all these variables. That can require a good deal of local knowledge and the only way to acquire this is time on the water. If your fishing schedule is very restricted, the best alternative is a professional guide or captain.

Fishing Mexico's Coronado Islands just south of San Diego is a good example. Before I started fishing these islands from my own boat, I had years of experience on the party boats where I tried to learn how the skippers fished the area. You have large rock formations, kelp beds and strong currents to contend with. The interplay of these factors coupled with the availability of food sources such as anchovies and squid have a dramatic effect on the fishery. Kelp bass, Pacific barracuda and bonito are frequent inhabitants of the area, but the main attraction are yellowtail and there is fierce competition among the party boats to record the best catches for their passengers. The few boats that consistently racked up the highest numbers were run by skippers who had an intimate knowledge of the area. A mere matter of yards in terms of where the boat was anchored often spelled the difference between mediocre fishing and a wide-open bite. In one particular spot, it was critical to try an anchor adjacent to an underwater ridge on an incoming tide. When the tide started to run, the resulting current would carry bait along the ridge and the yellows would be in hot pursuit. I hooked a lot of yellows from that spot in my own boat, but even with 20-pound-test tippets and 12-weight rods, most of the time I never got close to even bringing the fish to color. I would estimate that probably 90% of the time the fish either cut me off in the rocks or tangled me in the kelp. In my bait-fishing days with conventional gear, 40-pound-test line was considered light for this area so you can imagine how the odds shifted in the yellow's favor when I picked up a fly rod. But if it weren't for the years of fishing the area with skippers who were willing to divulge some of this information, I would have never been in a position to present my flies to these fish.

Regardless of the coast you fish on, one sure way of locating fish-attracting underwater structure is to key in on lobster-pots buoys. Just like many of our favorite species, lobster love structure. Lobstermen know this and set their traps according. The water depths can vary but generally the pots are set anywhere from 20 to 120 feet. You have to understand of course, that the buoys give an approximate location. First of all, the traps are generally not set directly atop the structure because of the risk of fouling. Besides, lobsters leave their rocky lairs at night scurrying over the bottom in search of a meal, making it unnecessary to set the pots right in the rocks. Secondly, just like anchor rope, the marker buoys are angled out away from the traps. To pinpoint the exact location of the bottom structure you'll need a good depth finder and recorder. However, if there are a lot of traps in the area, you can simply drift through the buoys. Dan Marini and his dad, affectionately known as "the chief," are absolute masters at picking their way through the maze of lobster pots and moored boats in their home waters off Chatham in Cape Cod. They know the area better than some people know their backyards and they have never failed to put me or my friends into striped bass.

Fishing from the shore poses its own set of challenges, but whether it's roosterfish off Baja or stripers at Martha's Vineyard, you'll need to read the beach. Many years ago, Jim Murray, the popular sports columnist for the *Los Angeles Times*, wrote an article about my early forays in the surf with fly-fishing tackle. He referred to me as the ultimate optimist. About a week after the piece was published, a colleague of mine at the university joined me on one of these outings. At the time, his fly-fishing experience was limited to fresh water. After his first dozen or so casts into waves that looked like crashing hilltops, he likened the experience to trying to ride a skateboard during an earthquake.

There's no doubt that the surf can be a formidable environment to fish regardless of the tackle choice. Crashing waves and grinding sand that can transform jagged rocks into billiard ball smoothness, undertows that suck the bottom out from under your feet, and wind that feels like the turbulence of a jet revving for takeoff, are all part of the scenario when you venture forth into the surf zone. But fleeting though it may be, fish do reside here. You just have to learn to read the signs that tell you when and where.

It's great to go fishing whenever you have the time, but particularly where the shoreline is concerned, you'll find that periods of optimum productivity are closely tied to tidal phases and you should plan your outings accordingly. Tidal currents must be reckoned with because they play such an important role in the availability of the fish's food sources. Incoming and strong spring tides (these occur when the earth, moon and sun are in alignment, exerting maximum gravitational pull on tidal flows) churn up the bottom, stirring up food items like small mollusks, sea worms and crabs. In rocky areas, the increased wave action knocks loose a variety of crustaceans and other marine organisms. Nature programmed the larger predator species to tune into these conditions, and that is why in many areas you will consistently experience the best action on incoming and outgoing tides. An hour before and an hour after the peak high tides can be some of the most productive periods to wet a line. I caught what is probably the first white sea bass on fly off of Guerro Negro in Baja fishing the beach on an incoming high tide. I logged many years fishing these beaches with conventional outfits using dead squid

as bait. Despite the fact that this is the sea bass's favorite food source (it has earned the name as the "candy bait"), my friends and I found that the vast majority of our hookups occurred during periods of moving water. During high-water and low-water slack periods, water movement is minimal, food sources are not being buffeted about and predators are reluctant to expend much energy looking for something that is not readily available. Realizing that these were very slow periods even when we were tossing bait, with fly gear I didn't even bother to fish. But as soon as the tide began to change, I would start casting in earnest. At the time, all my friends who were fishing Baja were confirmed conventional tackle anglers, but they always liked to see me do my thing with fly gear. I sacrificed catching a lot of fish that were more than eager to take bait, but persistence paid off and I finally enticed a white sea bass to eat what most good fly-tiers would consider a very poor squid imitation. More importantly, the bass were motivated to eat because the tide was right and my less-than-artistic creation looked like easy pickings.

However, knowing the right tide was only part of the equation. I had to have some knowledge of what section of beach would be the most promising. Experienced trout fishermen stress the necessity of learning to read a stream. The same applies to the surf. For someone who is new to this type of fishing, most stretches of beach may look basically the same. But veteran surf fishermen, like experienced surfers, know that this is not the case. The behavior of fish is closely associated with the nature of their habitat. It follows then, that when you begin to learn about the physical makeup of their environment, you are on your way to becoming a more accomplished angler. Some stretches of beach-front may be like the proverbial Dead Sea. The area is devoid of life, or at least the forms fishermen are interested in. But only a few yards away, there might be large concentrations of hungry predators waiting to ambush your offerings. To find these schools requires an ability to interpret the various signs of the surf.

Fundamentally, reading the surf involves the ability to interpret the characteristics of waves as they roll toward shore. This will give you an idea of what the bottom configuration is like. The key to much of this is related to the principal that waves tend to break over shallow bottoms. In contrast, they roll over deeper areas represented by depressions or troughs in the bottom. What this means is that the behavior of a wall of water as it makes its way toward the beach is an indication of the type of bottom that lies below. Imagine you are standing on a beach, or better yet, a pier because of the heightened visibility. What would you look for? If you observe what appears to be a relatively flat section of water rushing toward shore with waves breaking on either side, that's an indication that there is a bottom depression under the flat area of water. These deeper pockets are generally good areas to fish because food sources are likely to be concentrated there. A host of tiny marine organisms like crabs, worms, and small baitfish that are unable to swim against strong currents are eventually swept into the calmer water found in the deeper pockets.

CAPTAIN JOE BLADOS

In Baja, anytime we found a beach that was bordered by high cliffs, before driving out on the sand, we would use the height to study the wave patterns. It was a lot easier to spot the holes and troughs this way than when you're standing on the beach eye level with the waves. When we made our way down to the beach, we knew exactly where we wanted to fish. That's how I caught my first white sea bass on fly in the surf. My late buddy Ron Rock, who pioneered much of the surf fishing on Baja's Pacific coast, took me to a spot he referred to as "Variety." I asked him why he chose that name, and he said that he caught so many different species of fish here, he thought variety was the most appropriate description. Corbina, kelp bass, halibut, yellowfin croaker, spotfin croaker, pargo, rays and the prized white sea bass all regularly fed off these beaches—and over the years with the exception of rays and spotfin, every one of them

went for my flies. The sea bass however, were hard to come by primarily because they typically did not feed in close to the beach and I had a difficult time reaching them with fly gear. At the time I was using an old Powell 10-weight rod that I bought from the old man himself when I met him at one of the tackle shows in the Bay area. My reel was equally vintage. I couldn't afford one of the few custom-crafted models available at the time, and even if I had one, I wouldn't have fished the Baja beaches with it. My old standby back then was a System 10 Scientific Anglers, direct drive. The rod I'm sorry to say was stolen, but the reel still sits in my tackle drawer and occasionally I fish it when I get nostalgic. This outfit, coupled with some primitive leadcore shooting heads that Harry Kime showed me how to rig, accounted for many fish from those Baja beaches.

As was often the case on these outings, in less than an hour at this particular spot, Ron had already connected with two nice sea bass that went for the dead squid. I was having a good time with the yellowfin croaker and occasional pargo, but I really wanted one of those whites. I had caught my share on spinning and conventional tackle, but never on fly. Ron was not one to pick up the fly rod, but he enjoyed watching me fish it and would usually holler louder than I did when I hooked up. This time was no exception. Pargo can pull with the best of them, but when the sea bass hit and started to take line, I knew I was onto a good fish. Ron started yelling, "Maybe it's the kind." I knew of course that he was referring to white sea bass. Every time he hooked one off the beach, he would say, "It's the kind." I had my hopes up, but in these waters you never can be sure what has taken your offering. However, there is a characteristic of struggling sea bass that distinguishes them from most of the other game fish you can hook off Baja beaches. Similar to billfish, the whites will often surface and blow out their stomach contents. When this fish finally stopped taking line, we could see it on the surface between wave sets and that's when I knew I finally had my white. Actually, a more accurate way of putting it is I knew I had hooked my first white. I still had to land it. Anytime you hook a decent-size fish off the beach, you must resist the temptation to try and muscle it onto the shore. Especially with fairly light class tippets, if you apply just a tad more pressure at the wrong time, the combination of pounding surf and undertow can easily break the line. What you want to do is try and use the waves to your advantage by surfing the fish in toward shore. Just like a surfer preparing to catch a wave, pull on the fish just before the wave begins to break and reel as fast as you can when the fish is driven toward the beach. If a receding wave pulls the fish away from shore, do not increase the resistance by trying to pull back in the oppo-

CAPTAIN JOE BLADOS

site direction. Be patient and let the surf have its way. The water turbulence and crashing waves will eventually tire the fish to the point where you can slide it up the beach.

When I finally succeeded in doing so I was elated and saddened at the same time. The silvery flanks of the sea bass glistened against the sand and the foam that collected around the edges of it fins seemed like an added touch from an artist. This fish was a long time in coming and I had a tremendous sense of satisfaction. On the other hand, the bass was exhausted. The faint pulsations of its gill covers and the gasping gestures from the jaw were sure signs that it was about to expire. I could have none of this. Just minutes before I was totally focused on trying to claim this magnificent creature from the formidable environment where we first made contact. Now all I could think about was reviving it so I could set it free. Normally I am very fastidious about my equipment and take special pains to avoid dropping it in the water or sand. At this point I could care less. The rod was tucked under my arm and the reel was dragging bottom like a dredge as I cradled the bass in my hands, working it back and forth in an effort to re-oxygenate its gills. Ever so slowly I could feel the fish begin to regain strength, but I was reluctant to let it go. These are shark-infested waters and it wasn't uncommon to see large hammerheads silhouetted in the curls of waves mere yards in front of where we were fishing. After all this effort I didn't want to see my prize become table fare. Finally the fish decided for itself. I couldn't maintain my grasp and it bolted from my hands leaving a cloud of sand particles as it slid beneath an incoming wave.

Another physical characteristic of a beach worth noting is the degree to which it slopes toward shore. As waves roll in, they eventually crest and break. By noting the distance of break from the shoreline, it's possible to determine if the beach slopes gradually or sharply. On steeply sloping beaches, waves tend to break close to the water's edge and there will often be troughs close to shore. Marine organisms and small baitfish tend to be concentrated here so this is where you want to place your casts between the cresting waves.

On Baja's northern beaches I've seen halibut the size of pillowcases cruising these troughs eating barred perch fry. An inch-and-a-half-long white Clouser or Deceiver stripped erratically through these shoreline depressions will definitely draw their attention. I took my largest fly-rod halibut casting to a trough that wasn't more than 20 feet in front of me on a stretch of beach a few miles south of Ensenada. At the time I was catching barred perch on small Crazy Charlie patterns I originally tied for bonefish. I saw two nice halibut slide through the trough in front of me and got off two good casts, but they weren't interested. When they disappeared into the foam, I took the time to change flies and tied on a white-and-green Clouser. The Charlies proved to be a more productive fly for the perch, but the halibut had my interest and I was hoping more were in the area. I don't know if it was one of the same fish I had seen earlier, but after about 10 minutes of fruitless casting, I spotted the dark outline of a doormat-size halibut swimming from my left. To get a good placement in the direction the fish was swimming, I ran a few yards to my right and made a cast. The water was only a few feet deep but there was a strong current and I didn't want the fly to rise above the fish's feeding level when I started retrieving it. The combination of weighted eyes and a lead-core shooting head helped keep the fly near the bottom and the halibut went for it as soon as it detected its movement about 10 feet in front of where it was swimming. The flattie measured 31 inches which probably would have made the record books. I'll never know because my friends and I had a beach BBQ that night and the halibut was the featured dish.

Though seemingly a world apart, striped bass also tend to frequent the troughs adjacent to steep sloping beaches. Three years ago fishing Nantucket Island with my friend Charlie Boillod, provided me with a very dramatic example. Charlie is one of those fortunate souls who has a house on the island and unlike most of the seasonal residents, he spends considerable time tossing flies in the fish-rich waters. This was my first time on the island and I could not have had a better introduction. Charlie has intimate knowledge of the island, and he wasted little time getting me into fish. Some of the best

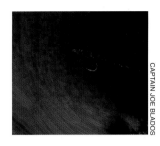

times were spent sight-fishing the flats from his Jones Brothers skiff which is about the most user-friendly, fly-fishing boat I've ever cast from. But Charlie is one of those well-rounded folks who likes to do it all and he suggested that we forego the convenience of the boat for one day and don the waders for a little shore fishing. I love to wade fish, but if I had access to that boat in these waters, I don't think I would be playing the role of foot soldier too often. However, I was his guest so I tried to display as much as enthusiasm as I could.

As is often the case in the Northeast, despite the fact that it was June, the morning started off cold and damp, but as we motored along the beach the dreary weather was no longer an issue. With their grassy dunes, wind-swept knolls and sugar-soft sand, the beaches here are as beautiful as anywhere I've ever been, and every stretch of shore looked like it would hold fish. Of course, despite the enticing appearance, that's not the case and Charlie knew what he wanted. When we pulled up to the spot he was looking for, I knew why he wanted to fish it. There was a long trough line etched with eel grass about 30 feet off the beach. Charlie was telling me about some of the big bass that were reported to be in this area when my attention was diverted by fish tearing up the surface about 200 feet from where we were parked. One ritual I dislike is the hassle of putting on chest-high waders. I hate it even more when there are fish breaking and I'm trying to get ready. At times like this, everything seems to go wrong. You have a difficult time sliding your foot into the neoprene legs, your socks are pushed down to your ankles, suspenders are tangled and snaps and buckles resist every attempt at fastening them. At least I had my fly-rod rigged and ready to go. Fortunately, by the time I finally got dressed, the bass were still there busting bait. The water was shallow and we could wade to within casting distance, but I forgot about the trough and almost went for a swim. My bad hip didn't help matters and Charlie's shouts to be careful went totally unheeded. I think I would have run through a mine field to get to those fish. I had on a Blados Crease Fly, Charlie was working a Clouser and within minutes we both were into school size stripers. The water in my waders and the twisted suspender sawing into my neck were no longer a bother. It was bass off the beach and it was heaven.

The action lasted about 20 minutes and as we started wading back in to shore, Charlie reminded me about the trough. I thought he was cautioning me to be careful and that's what I focused on as I picked my way through some rocks and eel grass. I always make it a point to wear polarized glasses because for one thing, they enable you to see the bottom when wading. In clear water they also help you spot fish, but for the log size bass that bolted in front of me, they would not have been necessary. Clearly, this was one of the largest stripers I have ever seen and it could not have been more than 10 feet from where I was walking. It was lying in the trough and I spooked it as I walked through. When I yelled, Charlie laughed and said, "I told you they were in here." I don't know if that bass would have gone for a fly before the area was disturbed, but it does confirm the fact that you should always pay special attention to trough lines along the beach.

Even when you have located productive stretches of beach, you can't expect that conditions will remain the same indefinitely. It's not that way offshore and it's certainly not the case along the shoreline. Like the old Greek philosopher observed, everything is in a constant state of flux. The influence of factors such as tides, currents, wind and storms at sea can re-sculpture the

beach in little more than a matter of hours. In practical terms this simply means that a spot that was productive one day may not be near as good the next. The best strategy is to resist becoming locked into one place. Be mobile and have a willingness to try different beaches and different stretches of coastline.

Almost every trip I made to the Pacific side of the Baja peninsula brought a different set of conditions. About the only factor that seemed to remain fairly constant was the slope of the beach. Aside from that, you couldn't assume that anything would be the same. A beach front that may have been clear the week before could be strewn with massive bundles of kelp the next time down making it impossible to fish. An area that had deep pockets one day might be flat as a runway the next. That's one reason why we always drove down with a 4-wheel-drive vehicle. Whether it's the Jersey shore or Baja, wherever you have access, these vehicles are a godsend to the shore-bound angler. You can literally cover the waterfront.

CHAPTER 7

Don't Leave Home Without It: Auxiliary Gear

First Aid

It may have something to do with the fact that my wife is an RN and a health fanatic, or that I have a number of friends who are doctors, or maybe it's simply that I'm older and a wee bit wiser. Whatever the case, now whenever I prepare for a fishing trip where I know that medical aid is not likely to be close at hand, I make first-aid items a priority. It wasn't always that way, but I do remember an incident many years ago when I just happened to be prepared.

Living in Southern California at the time, I didn't put much stock in the old saying that "March comes in like a lamb and goes out like a lion." I thought that only applied to areas like the Northeast where there are definite seasonal changes. I was wrong. It was the end of March but for almost a week there were a series of Pacific storms that pounded the southland coast bringing lots of rain and heavy surf. This was back in the days when the bonito fishing was nothing short of phenomenal in King Harbor and March was traditionally one of the most productive months. I'm sure today there are any number of anglers who would gladly pay hundreds of dollars just for the privilege of casting from the breakwater to experience the kind of action that I came to expect as a normal state of affairs. The action on bonito may have been commonplace but I never took it for granted and I made it a priority to fish for them every chance I got. Since I lived within walking distance of the Redondo breakwater, I had plenty of opportunity. True to form, the first day with no rain, I made plans to fish that afternoon.

The portion of the weather report I listened to was dead accurate concerning the break in the

Studded gloves make handling fish a lot easier.

storm. There was a cloudless sky and the visibility was unlimited. What I didn't pay attention to was the fact that the surf was still running strong and high. Truthfully, this fact probably would not have deterred me from going out. In thirty-some years of scrambling over this breakwater, I learned every rock formation and picking my path through the boulders became as routine as driving to work. If waves started crashing over the rocks, I knew where I could shield myself among the crevices. I also got in the habit of constantly looking behind me. I always tell beginning fly-fishers to watch their back casts. In fishing the breakwater with the open ocean at your back, glancing behind you to monitor the wave action is an added safety measure.

No doubt due to the heightened wave action that day, there weren't many people on the rocks but there was one guy, obviously unconcerned, who was fishing the lower part of the break wall out near the end of the jetty. The rest of us at least were standing where the rocks were piled high and this afforded some measure of protection. But even here we were getting wet when the occasional big one came crashing in showering us with spray that hit like a fire hose.

At first I had no idea a really big roller was heading in. My first clue was when I saw the guy way off to my right running toward me. Immediately I turned around and saw this mountain of water coming our way. I yelled to the guy to get down between the rocks. There was no way he was going to make it to higher ground before the wave broke. I didn't even try retrieving my line. I lowered my rod, jumped off the rock I was standing on, and wedged myself into a crevice between two large boulders. I heard the wall of water hit the rocks and then instantly felt like a football coach who gets dowsed with one of those large water containers. I was soaked, but I wasn't hurt. Unfortunately that was not the case for the guy who was trying to run to safety. I never saw him get hit, but it was obvious he got pounded. In the five minutes it took for me to make my way over to him, the blood oozing through his water-soaked clothes made him look in a lot worse shape than he actually was. He was lucky that the cuts and scrapes were only superficial, but he wasn't quite out of the woods on this one. The rocks are caked with bird droppings and if you fell and cut yourself, the wound became immediately infected. I had been through this many times before. Even though this was in the days before shin splints and a hip replacement, notwithstanding my agility on the rocks, I inevitably fell victim to cuts and scrapes. I would wash the wounds with saltwater and continue fishing. I

never took any of this seriously until I woke up one morning and saw that my throbbing knee was the size of a grapefruit. I had to go to my doctor and he put me on antibiotics. He told me that this was not something to be taken lightly and that if I didn't want to go through this again, I should carry a bottle of hydrogen peroxide to immediately cleanse any open wounds. I took his advice and I like to think that this fellow who looked like he had rubbed up against a giant cheese shredder, also benefited. Since then, whenever I put together a first-aid kit for a trip that is going to involve considerable distance from any medical facilities, I make it a practice to include a plastic bottle of hydrogen peroxide.

Always have a well-stocked first-aid kit onboard.

Of course, if you know beforehand that access to medical supplies isn't going to be a problem, then you don't have to be as thorough in this regard. This is how it's been for me on my trips to Casa Mar in Costa Rica. Having fished there for so many years, I know that Bill Barnes has a supply of just about anything you'll ever need. Living there on a full-time basis, it's to his own personal benefit to have everything close at hand. In addition, he has a large contingent of physician friends who are constantly bringing him updated medications and other medical items that they want immediate access to if they ever need it. I remember two occasions down there when his medical inventory averted potential tragedies.

One incident involved my friend Ed Ow. Ed was the founder and publisher of what was a truly high-quality fishing publication known as *Angler* magazine. By giving me a writing assignment on Costa Rica, it was Ed who initiated my introduction to Bill Barnes and Casa Mar. On one of the many trips we eventually made there together, we traveled about two hours up the Rio Colorado River to a small village where we bought live prawns for the evening meal. Ed saw a set of jaws that came from what was obviously a very large bull shark and asked the fisherman if he wanted to sell them. "That is what they are here for," he replied in Spanish, and Ed made the transaction. The fellow wrapped them in a plastic bag and Ed placed the jaws on the boat deck near where he was seated. This proved to be a very bad spot to store them.

On our way back to the lodge we stopped to do some fishing. We hit a productive snook hole and in the excitement of hooking and playing these fish, Ed completely forgot about the jaws. When he stepped to the side to give the guide room to reach over the gunwale and release a snook, Ed stepped on the jaws. In seconds the white plastic bag was covered in blood. About 20 minutes later when we arrived at the lodge, the boat deck looked like the bloodied floor of a big-city emergency room on a busy Saturday night. At least Ed had two things working in his favor. Number one was the fact that Bill had all the necessary medications and dressings. Secondly, there was a psychiatrist in camp. I recall him saying something to the effect that the last open wound he treated was on a cadaver in medical school. Nonetheless, he was the most qualified in these matters and he took care of Ed before he was flown out to the hospital the next morning in San Jose.

The second injured party wasn't a human, but Bill regarded it as such. It was his prized bird dog, Playboy. When you travel to a place like Casa Mar with all the amenities and the creature comforts we tend to take for granted, it's easy to lose sight of the nature of the surrounding environment. If you live in or around a major city in the U.S., in many respects you are probably safer at a place like Casa Mar than you are at home. It is true that in a rainforest jungle there are wild critters roaming about that can be far more threatening than some neighbor's unfriendly dog. However, after more than three decades of fishing places like this, I can tell you that the chances of a direct encounter are very slim. It took me almost 25 years to get lucky enough to photograph a jaguar standing in a clearing. Nevertheless, you still have to be careful and exercise a little common sense. For example, I would not be especially fond of swimming in the river. I certainly would not want to frolic along its banks at night. The once fearsome shark

population has been significantly depleted, but there are numerous large saltwater crocodiles and caiman are very common. By day, both species tend to be wary of humans, at least when you try to approach them by boat. At night on foot, it could be an entirely different ballgame. Poor Playboy found out the hard way.

Soon after the sun goes down, caiman and crocodiles like to swim in close to the riverbank where they sometimes lie with their heads partially out of the water. The first time I shone a light into the river early one evening, I was amazed at how many eyes dotted the coal-black surface. It's an eerie feeling. Playboy was also aware of their presence and no one seemed particularly concerned when he would run down to the boat dock and bark at

Billy Pate with one of the countless sailfish he's subdued on fly tackle.

his jagged-toothed neighbors. That all changed one night after dinner. A bunch of us were sitting around the lounge area when we heard the dog's barks suddenly shift into a series of shrieks. Bill was the first one out the door. Bad knees and all, he outran everyone to the boat dock. What we saw at first didn't seem real. It looked like something out of a movie. A large crocodile had the dog's mid-section clenched between its jaws. Before any of us could react, the foreman's old German shepherd bolted onto the scene and began tearing at the crocodile's tail. It was clear that this reptile predator from some ancient past did not want to relinquish its prize, but after repeated blows with an oar and the nonstop annoyance of the shepherd, it finally dropped the dog and slid back into the water.

It did not seem like it at the time, but Playboy was one lucky dog. Bill cradled him in his arms and walked him over to the dining room where we got our first clear look at the kind of damage this overgrown lizard can inflict. The poor dog had a series of puncture wounds that looked like they had been made by gaff handles. In an incredible stroke of good fortune, "Dr. Joe," a general surgeon and a close friend of Bill's, had just flown in the day before. He cleaned and closed all the wounds and Bill had the dog bird hunting six months later. But even with "Dr. Joe" on hand, the dog would have certainly died if the necessary medical supplies were not available.

On a recent trip to Florida where my wife and I went fishing with Corbett Davis, Jr., Corbett's diligence regarding his boat's first-aid kit and my wife's training as an RN both proved invaluable. The fishing was a little slow in his home waters off Pensacola so we planned to trailer his Maverick to Fort Morgan, Alabama. In the process of loading the boat on the trailer Corbett slipped on the launch ramp and sliced his arm above the elbow on some barnacles. He had an appointment with a dermatologist early that morning and had the doctor take a look at his arm. She saw that it was a nasty cut and advised Corbett that he should probably have it stitched. However when it comes to fishing, Corbett borders on fanaticism and he asked the doctor to bandage the wound so we could continue on our way. The plan was to fish the oil platforms off Fort Morgan, but we didn't have to run that far because fish were breaking only a couple of miles outside the harbor. There were Spanish mackerel mixed with fast-moving schools of rampaging false albacore. Corbett hooked into one of the albacore and I started snapping photos. I quickly stopped when Kathy yelled that there was blood all over the deck and gunwales. The exertion of pulling on that fish caused the wound to re-open and despite Kathy's protests Corbett continued to fight the fish until he had it boat side. I wanted to cut the leader but he insisted that I remove the fly. That ate up about 30 seconds and blood was already beginning to pool on deck. Of course, I never thought about it beforehand and when Kathy yelled for the first-aid kit I immediately shot the question to Corbett. I felt a small sense of relief when he answered, "it's in the rear seat compartment." I felt even better when I lifted a large green box that was marked, "First Aid." In addition to a full complement of bandages, there was a large bottle of peroxide that Kathy soon emptied with repeated dowsing over the wound. The only trouble was that the expiration date had long since passed. She managed to stop the bleeding and we spent the remainder of the day in the local ER. The doctor there told us that the major problem in an injury like this is the likelihood of infection. Barnacle wounds can be especially serious because barnacles accumulate all sorts of pollutants.

What I've learned from all this is that you don't have to pack like a paramedic, but for your own protection and the safety of others who may be accompanying you, there are a number of basic first-aid items that you should have readily available. Obviously, if you have any special medical issues, you should consult with a physician to make sure that you'll have everything you'll need. And to help guard against the possibility of making things worse than they are, it also makes good sense to get a doctor's advice concerning the use of any first-aid items you carry with you.

In addition to the hydrogen peroxide which is basically a disinfectant rinse intended for immediate external application, you want some type of antiseptic like Neosporin to help prevent infection after the wound is initially cleaned. Band-Aids in a variety of sizes should be an integral part of any first-aid kit. For large cuts, a physician friend recommends the butterfly Steri Strips because they function almost like stitches in holding sections of skin together. Three-inch gauze wrap secured by Transpor tape is also very useful to help keep pressure on a wound.

Many people mistakenly think that heat is good for an injury. In some cases it is, but when in doubt, the rule of thumb is to apply ice. Ice is indispensable for swelling, pain and inflammation and an easy way to always have it close at hand is to carry it in the form of chemical cold packs like the ones often used in hospitals. The pack is activated when it's struck against a solid surface. In conjunction with ice, an Ace-wrap is a very handy item if you have to stabilize something like a wrist or ankle.

Anything you don't want to get wet, like special medications or matches, should be secured in a waterproof package or container. A friend of mine had a very thorough first-aid kit that he always carried on his boat, but he made the mistake of stowing it in a large canvass bag. One day when we were fishing calico bass at Catalina Island, we were closer to shore than we should have been and a wave crashed over the transom. The self-bailing cockpit and the fact that the outboard was still running prevented a major disaster. But after we got squared away, we found that the canvass bag and just about everything in it were soaked. Most of the first-aid items had to be discarded. The few things that remained dry had been previously stored in plastic zip-lock bags. These bags are some of the handiest storage containers you'll ever find. I pack all kinds of things in them, from pre-tied leaders to flies.

Sun Protection

Traditionally most folks never assigned suntan cream the same degree of importance as other first-aid items, but in light of the medical profession's warnings about the dangers of overexposure, this is beginning to change. Because of the intensifying effect of the sun being reflected off the water, everyone who fishes should take extra precaution in this regard. Suntan creams and lotions have a sun protection factor (SPF) rating printed on the container and the advice I've been given by several dermatologists is to use those with high ratings in the 15 to 25 category. In terms of clothing choices, dark colors afford the best protection.

Perhaps the one area of our body that is most vulnerable are the eyes. As fishermen, we want polarizing lenses to give us better vision into the water, but more importantly, sunglasses help prevent damage to our eyes. A good rule of thumb here is to choose sunglasses that are dark enough so you can't see your eyes when looking in a mirror.

Once you acquire a good pair, you want to make sure you don't lose them, so some type of leash or cord is highly recommended. I lost about four pair of prescription polarids before I finally saw the light (no pun intended) and began using a cord that looped around my neck. Even though I knew it served a good purpose, for years I resisted doing so because it reminded me of some of the elderly ladies who worked in the school library. Now I'm no longer so concerned with making a fashion statement but accidents still happen and for that reason, it's prudent to always have an extra pair on hand. If you wear prescription lenses this can get expensive but there are alternatives that can save you some money. One way to go is to use clip-on lenses. With the new pair of glasses I was buying from my optometrist, I made sure there were polarized clip-on lenses available that would fit over the frame and had him order me a pair. Some people have complained that the clips can be blown off when running fast in an open boat but I have yet to have this

A well-equipped van for fishing the beach.

happen. A second, and perhaps better alternative, is to buy a pair of polarized glasses that fit over your prescription pair. I did this while on a trip to Martha's Vineyard last summer. When I arrived on the island, I realized that I only had one pair of prescription polarids with me. I was in Larry's Tackle Shop chatting with Moe Flaherty, one of the Vineyard's top guides, and he recommended that I try a pair of FitOvers he had sitting on the counter. These glasses do just what the name says, they fit right over your regular glasses. Two days later back in his shop, I asked Moe if he was psychic. He asked me what I meant and I told him I dropped my prescription glasses overboard that morning fishing Dogfish Bar with his partner John Cherchio. I think John was more upset than I was, but I wasn't too concerned because I had the FitOvers and my regular pair of prescription glasses. I've been using the FitOvers for the past year and I like them. If you're going to fish past sunset, all you have to do is remove the FitOvers and fish with your standard prescription glasses.

For most daylight conditions, a baseball type cap is an ideal complement to polarized sunglasses. The cap's brim reduces the sun's glare and if you're trying to spot fish, this will help you see them better. The only problem with this type of cap is when you're traveling in an open boat. If statistics where kept on such incidents, I think I would hold some kind of record for having the most hats blown off in a given season. The sad thing about this is that there's a simple solution similar to the one used for preventing your glasses from falling overboard. All you have to do is wear a lanyard to clip the cap to a jacket or shirt collar. These are available in most fly shops. So why haven't I been using one? I don't like the way they look. Appearance-wise I've already compromised with the eyeglass lanyard, and I get my caps free.

Appropriate Clothing

Working our way from head to toe, proper foot gear will help you avoid "the agony of the feet." Personally, whenever conditions permit, I like to fly-fish barefoot. Even after all these years, I still have a tendency to stand on the line more than I should and when I'm barefoot, at least sometimes I can tell when I'm doing it. However, even when conditions may appear safe, going barefoot can invite injury. My good friend Larry Merly is a very experienced fly-fisherman. He makes his home in Connecticut but has logged a lot of time fishing in the tropics so he's very aware of the hazards of sunburn. On a trip we made together to fish stripers on the flats with Paul Dixon, Larry took all the necessary precautions except for one mistake. About mid morning, the temperature began to climb and he took his shoes and socks off. In only a few hours time his feet looked like cooked lobsters. Early that morning when he applied the suntan cream to his face, neck and hands, he had his shoes on. But when he removed them, he completely forgot about the exposed skin on the topside of his feet and he ended up with a painful sunburn.

As Bob Popovics found out, sunburn isn't the only misfortune that can befall unprotected feet. We were on Joe Blados' Maverick flats boat, and it was Bob's turn to take his shot on the bow platform. When he took a step to try and spot a fish that Joe had pointed to, his big toe caught the U-shaped fitting that is used to hold the push pole in place. To avoid catching lines (and feet) these clips are designed so that you can push them flush into the gunwale. Unfortunately, it wasn't in the recessed position and a chunk of Bob's toe was impaled on the corner edge. It was weeks before Bob could put shoes on.

On Baja's East Cape beaches, fishing barefoot is very tempting particularly in the summer months when the temperatures can really soar, but you have to be careful. One day I stepped on a small Portuguese man-o-war jellyfish that had washed up on shore. It was about the size of a golf ball and I never saw it, but I certainly felt it. The sensation was like stepping on a hot iron. Another little critter that can ruin your vacation is the spine-armored blowfish. These are plentiful on the East Cape and they wash up on shore in the hundreds. Even when dead and dried up, some of their spines remain pointed up and you're in for a very bad time if you step on one barefoot.

If you are concentrating on where you are walking, you can often spot these hazards well in advance of stepping on them. But generally when fishing, your focus is elsewhere and it's easy to plant your foot on something you definitely want to avoid. Three summers ago down there I spotted fish breaking off the beach about 50 yards from where I was casting. I was running to the spot when my pace was suddenly interrupted by an abrupt change in my footing. I had the unpleasant experience of stepping on a section of rotting seal carcass. It was as slimy as motor oil on a smooth cement floor and I went flying into the beach headfirst. Flies and leaders were scattered everywhere and my reel was choked with sand. At least I wasn't hurt and the water was close by so I could wash off. When I went back to the carcass to gather up my gear, I could see a few broken rib bones jutting out from the jelly-like mass. If one of those had pierced my foot I could have been in for the mother of all infections, so I considered myself lucky. I also resolved to no longer go barefoot on these beaches. If there is a lot of coral or jagged rocks, I wear neoprene flats boots like the ones offered by Simms. These are lightweight boots that have breathable uppers. The zippers are rust proof, but to help prevent sand from clogging the zipper track, I use a pair of gravel guards. When fishing places where I don't need ankle protection, I wear low-cut neoprene booties popularly referred to as water walkers. Like the neoprene boots, these are designed for wet wear, so even in places like Baja, you can cool off simply by wading into the water. In more northern climates, if the weather isn't too cold, these boots and booties are ideal when fishing from boats. There are no laces to tangle the fly line and the mid-sole designs provide a safe grip on slippery surfaces like boat decks.

However, footgear does not make you invincible, a fact that a deckhand friend of mine found out the hard way. One day on Farnsworth Bank off Catalina Island we were fishing sculpin. Normally these fish are caught in deep water, but he told me that his skipper found a spot near the bank where the fish were concentrated at about 35 feet. My friend knew that I always wanted to take a sculpin on fly, so he invited me out to give it a try. It was a weekday, the passenger load was light, and I had the bow area all to myself. Using a lead-core shooting head,

I started hitting a few fish, but my cast-catch ratio wasn't anything near what the bait guys were doing. They were fishing with pieces of squid and it seemed like every bait that slipped below the surface was taken in a matter of seconds. There were a lot of fish coming aboard and since sculpin are very tasty, most of them were not being released. Instead, following standard practice on the party boats, there were stored in potato sacks that were hung on hooks along the sides of the large aft bait tank.

We probably hadn't been at the spot for more than a half hour and the sacks were bulging with fish. My friend was wearing shin-high rubber deck boots and he kicked one of the sacks to make a little room at the bait tank. Seconds later he fell to the deck like he was hit with a knockout punch from a prizefighter. At first I didn't realize what the problem was, but the skipper knew immediately. He yelled for everyone to reel their lines in and told the other deckhand to start pulling the anchor. It was clear he wanted to get back to the dock as quickly as possible. He pulled the boot off my friend's foot and immersed his toes in a bucket of ice. My friend was in terrible pain and all he could say was, "I should have known better."

The dorsal and pectoral fins on sculpin pack a powerful venom and when he kicked the sack, one of the spines went through the boot right into his foot. Paramedics were waiting at the dock and he was rushed to the hospital. Fortunately the venom didn't do any permanent damage and my friend was back on the boat two weeks later. Now he wears steel-toed boots and confines his kicking to soccer balls.

One of our more flamboyant presidents made the now-famous statement about walking softly. I would add the word carefully, particularly when you're fishing afoot in unfamiliar terrain. On the second day of what turned out to be one of the most miserable trips I ever experienced, I found myself stuck waist deep in muck. I was at Drake's Bay on Costa Rica's Pacific coast. I made the mistake of trusting some folks I didn't know very well and ended up staying at a place that could have passed for the Tico version of the Bates Motel. The only person who knew anything about fishing the area was a young kid who had access to an ancient skiff and outboard. The first day out we had great fishing near Canos Island, but the motor was on its last legs and I didn't want to chance going out again. A small cove about a mile from where we were staying looked like it could be a productive spot so I set off to do some shore fishing. I was wearing a pair of strap-on thongs and they proved ideal for the type of tropical terrain in which I

was walking. Everything was fine until I reached the mangroves. As a kid I hated track, especially the high jump, and trying to traverse the giant roots reminded me of those loathsome leg lifts that I never seemed to master. At least I was making some progress at my own pace without the annoyance of a storm trooper coach yelling at you. When I reached a clearing about 25 yards from the shoreline, I thought I had it made. Not so. I walked about ten feet and the ground suddenly gave way. When the pudding-like ooze climbed no further than the elastic waistband on my shorts, I felt a sense of relief. The first thought that came to mind when I hit the soft spot was quicksand and I envisioned myself being swallowed up like some doomed character in a Tarzan movie.

Now my problem was extricating myself. I still had hold of my fly outfit and for a brief moment I considered the possibility of casting the fly to one of the mangrove roots to pull myself out with the fly line. Of course looking back on this, it's easy to see what a dumb idea it was. But in partial defense, I would like to say that even though I wasn't panicked, I was in a very unpleasant set of conditions and I wanted to get the hell out as quickly as possible, so at the time this didn't seem too far fetched. That option quickly faded when I pulled the reel out of the muck. Though far less appetizing, it bore a strange resemblance to the fudge-dipped ice cream balls I used to concoct at my father's soda fountain. The thought made me laugh and a little humor at that point was a good thing. The reel was so caked in mud that I couldn't even see the fly line and there was no way the spool was going to turn so I couldn't pull any line off anyway.

I did not relish the next option, but it was the only way I was going to free myself. I couldn't lift my legs because the thongs were acting like suction cups in the mud. My next move came right out of a Navy Seal training film and now it was my turn to put it into practice. I shut my eyes as tight as I could then bent over and buried my head in the muck. This enabled me to get my hands down to my feet so I could loosen the straps and work my feet out of the thongs. Before plunging my head in I had the sense to study the path to the shoreline because I did not want to open my eyes until I could wash myself off in the water. I remember thinking this was like fraternity hell night and as I had done way back then, I tried to blunt my sensibilities to the misery at hand and just focus on the immediate goal of plunging ahead. It probably took less than a minute, but as you know, time has a way of dragging when you're in a place or situation you wish to leave behind as quickly as possible. With my feet free of the thongs I was able to make forward progress and gradually I found firm footing. Finally, I was able to stand up on solid ground and it was almost like being on land after weeks at sea. But the sensation that stands out most vividly in my mind was getting into the water. It's interesting how radical contrasts in our experiences have a way of significantly implanting our memory bank and I will never forget the

Corbett Davis, Jr. releasing a nice jack near his home waters off Pensacola.

magnitude of the relief I felt when I first waded into the water. The temperature in that little cove was probably in the high seventies but it felt as refreshing as a fast-moving stream in the remote Sierras. I laid in the water like a poolside tourist in Palm Springs and almost lost sight of the fact that the purpose of this arduous trek was to fish. I eventually got around to that and caught a couple of snook. It was the hardest pair of fish I ever worked for.

Far removed from this tropical climate was another misstep, this time in the cold Klamath River in Northern California. This time it wasn't really my fault. I had the services of a guide and it was his directions that landed me in the water. There were three of us fishing and he told us to work our way down stream. "Cast, retrieve and walk to your right," was the way he put it. That seemed reasonable enough. After all, he was the guide

and we all assumed he knew this stretch of river. Unfortunately for me, that proved erroneous. It was my misfortune to be on the far right and after a series of casts and moves, when I stepped right, there was no place to plant my foot.

My friend who was fishing to my left saw what was happening, but he couldn't reach my left hand in time to pull me back to higher ground. Suddenly I was totally immersed in the river and for the first few seconds I was gripped with the fear of being pulled under by the current. When that didn't materialize, I relaxed and just let myself go for a ride downstream. I was wearing a pair of chest-high neoprene waders and was thankful that I had them cinched tight around my waist with a wading belt. Water spilled in over my shoulders but for the most part, the boots remained dry and I floated downstream in an upright position. The guide immediately jumped into the drift boat and started rowing furiously in my direction but by the time he reached me, I had already beached myself on a sandbar.

It was around 9:00 a.m. which was still too early for the sun's rays to bathe the floor of the steep canyon along the river where we were fishing. Things could have been much worse if it were mid winter, but given the chilly morning air and the fact that the water temperature was somewhere in the low 50s, I started to get cold to the point of having the shakes. It didn't make me feel much better when the guide started taking about the dangers of hypothermia, especially since it was his misjudgment that got me into this predicament in the first place. I will say this for him, he sure knew how to build a fire. The roaring blaze coupled with the spare dry clothes my friends and I brought along, gradually eased me back in to the comfort zone. It isn't necessary to have a complete wardrobe, but anytime you're on or near the water, and are a long distance from warmth and shelter, an extra set of dry clothes can be a godsend.

Regardless of where you are fishing, one clothing item you never want to be without is rain gear, but it's surprising how many people I run into who are not carrying a set. Especially around bodies of water, weather can change quickly, so even if the day looks great, do not assume it will remain that way for the duration of your outing. Ed Ow and I both made that mistake one time at Casa Mar. At least the consequences weren't as severe as the shark jaw incident I referred to a few pages back. Casa Mar is located in a rainforest jungle, so this should tell you something. Nevertheless, it was a beautiful, cloudless, sunny morning and we didn't think we would need the rain suits. The guide, by the way, had his. They always do. Anyway, as it turned out, in most areas the day remained bright and sunny, except for the spot upriver where we were fishing. The sky darkened as if evening suddenly descended and the rain came in torrents. When the guide fired up the outboard to take us back to the lodge, the added speed with which we hit the pellets of rain actually stung our exposed skin. Back at the lodge everything was clear and we found out that we were the only ones who got caught in a downpour.

Tools of the Trade

When I was wheeled into the operating room for my hip surgery, to ease my anxiety somewhat, I jokingly remarked to my surgeon that it looked like he had enough tools on hand to build a house. He smiled down on me and said, "You wouldn't want me to embark on this venture without being totally prepared." Of course the consequences would be a lot less dramatic, but days later lying in bed recuperating, I was thinking how the issue of preparedness can also effect the outcomes of our fishing experiences. As a take-off on a once-popular commercial, I have this chapter title, "don't leave home without it," written across a supply box that I always pack along with my fishing gear. The items in that box may be considered supplemental, but in countless instances they've played a critical part in the overall success and satisfaction of my fishing trips.

It's difficult to rank these items in the order of importance, but if I had to choose the handiest fishing tool it would be pliers. They can serve endless functions like flattening barbs, removing hooks, bending wire, cutting line (I prefer nail clippers for closely trimming knots), turning nuts, screws, whatever, I would be lost without them. Personally, I do not like wearing a pair on my belt which is probably the most convenient way to carry them, but I always make sure they are readily accessible. I also keep them well lubricated so you don't have to be a champion arm wrestler to open and close them.

A sheepshead from the Louisiana bayous.

Next to properly tied knots, I tend to be compulsive about keeping my hooks razor sharp, so I regard a file as an indispensable part of my auxiliary gear. I'm amazed at how many good guides tend to be negligent in this respect. In the cases where they do have a file on hand, many times they're useless because they are either rusted or the grooves are clogged with filings. To prevent that, I also keep the file well lubricated and I carry a small wire brush to clean it. Lefty showed me a neat way of warding off rust. He cuts two strips from an old leather belt the length of the file. Then he saturates both strips with oil. He places the file between the two strips and binds them together with duct tape. Now you a holster that continually lubricates the file. I criticized a guide friend of mine for the abysmal state of his file and he told me that it was his job to put me on the fish, not to keep my hooks sharp. I don't know how many guides share this opinion, but if you have a good file on hand, you don't have to worry about it.

Duct tape and a small pair of scissors are also two items that seem to have an almost infinite variety of uses and they're easy to pack. I've used the tape to bind everything from torn waders to bothersome boat cleats and scissors will perform cutting operations that would be impractical or impossible with nail clippers or pliers.

Though I don't use them as often as some of the other items mentioned, sewing needles can come in mighty handy. I use them for tying speed nail knots, picking out wind knots, removing splinters and even for their intended purpose of stitching clothing. Don't forget to bring along some thread, not only for sewing but also to use in conjunction with a fly-tying bobbin. Even if you do not plan on tying flies, a bobbin and thread is useful for wrapping on rod guides and tiptops. In addition to some melt-type glue for tiptops, a fly-tying bobbin and thread are a part of my emergency rod-repair kit. Of course, such a kit wouldn't be very useful without spare guides and tiptops and if you're fishing far from home, it's good insurance to have some of these on hand. Snake guides usually aren't a problem because these are wrapped onto the rod. Tiptops, on the other hand, are designed to fit over the rod tip and if the rod is broken below the very top, the taper may make it difficult to fit a new tiptop guide. One way to get around this is instead of trying to fit the guide over the broken top of the rod, flatten the hollow portion of the guide with pliers and then wrap the guide to the rod shaft. Cosmetically, it may not look too good, but at least you'll be able to fish the rod until a more permanent repair can be made.

A small flashlight is also an important part of my auxiliary tackle repertoire. On that ill-fated trip to Drake's Bay, in addition to the mud fiasco, I suffered a bad insect bite when I reached inside my shaving kit one night to fetch a couple of aspirins. It was never determined what kind of insect it was that nailed me, but my hand swelled and when I returned home I had to go to a specialist in tropical medicine who treated me with an aggressive regime of powerful antibiotics. I learned two things from that incident. One is to always keep my bags zipped closed whenever I'm in a place where unwelcome critters can crawl or slither into my personal belongings. Secondly, I now make it a practice to use a light before plunging my hand into dark places.

Of course if you fish at night you definitely will need a light, but you have to be judicious in how you use it. Contrary to what many people believe, a large, bright light is generally not a good choice. First of all, a bright-intensity light can temporarily impair your vision when you turn it off because your eyes will take longer to adjust to the sudden darkness. Secondly a bright light will typically draw the wrath of fellow anglers if you're fishing stripers off the beach because it can put fish off their feeding mode.

There are a number of quality flashlights designed for shorebound anglers. One model that I particularly like is the Buck Light that was recommended to me by Moe Flaherty. Moe has a wealth of experience prowling the beaches at night so I listened to what he had to say. This flashlight is compact, it uses two triple-A batteries, it's water resistant with two rubber O-rings around the lens, it has a pen-style clip making it easy to affix to your clothing and a hole at the top end so you have the option of wearing it around your neck with a lanyard.

Many people have given up smoking, but matches or, better yet, a good lighter are very handy items to have around. In a pinch, matches can substitute for a failed flashlight. In a wilderness setting they can be a lifesaver.

The Stripping Basket

It's one of the most functional auxiliary items a fly-fisher can have on hand. It's virtually maintenance free, it's easy to make your own and it's inexpensive. As far as a piece of fly-fishing equipment is concerned, I can't think of an item that has more going for it than a stripping basket, yet surprisingly there are many anglers who stubbornly refuse to use one. That's unfortunate and I can cite a litany of sad tales where the lack of a basket proved to be a significant handicap.

A brief review of the basics will help underscore the importance of a stripping basket. Remember that in fly-fishing the reel plays no part in the cast. Unlike a conventional revolving spool reel or spinning reel where the line comes off the spool during the cast, in fly-fishing the length of line you wish to cast is pulled from the spool by hand. In addition, the reel is not used to retrieve line after each cast. Instead, line is gathered in by hand, a technique referred to as stripping. So if a guide yells at you to strip, you probably shouldn't start removing your clothes.

OK, if the line is pulled off the spool prior to the cast and isn't wound back on the reel, where does it go? Well, you don't have to be a physicist to deduce that the line will fall at your feet on the ground, the deck, the beach or wherever you happen to be standing. Usually if the surface is clutter free, you don't have much to worry about. But that isn't always the case. About ten years ago I made a trip to Columbia to fish a place called Bahia Tebada. It was situated in a remote rainforest jungle, but the accommodations were clean and comfortable and the skiffs were seaworthy and immaculately maintained. They were custom built with fly-fishing in mind with large open decks that were free of the usual obstacles that can play havoc with your fly line. As I always do, I packed a stripping basket along with my other gear, but after looking at the skiffs my first afternoon at the lodge, I felt that I wouldn't need it. The first hour of fishing the next morning went fine, but as the day wore on I found that my new fly line started to deteriorate. The line became very sticky and then the coating began to peel off. Eventually the telltale odor of fuel tipped me off to the source of my problem. A fuel leak developed and gas was trickling out on deck. We tried washing down the deck with sea water, but the fuel continued to ravage the fly line and by the end of the day it was completely ruined. Mishaps like this are one reason you always want to pack extra fly lines. But if I had used my stripping basket, the line would never have made contact with the deck and there would not have been a problem.

It isn't often that you will be fortunate enough to be standing on a surface that is completely free of line-snagging obstacles. Even when I'm giving a casting demonstration indoors and the surface is perfectly flat and clean as a refinished ice rink, I find that from time to time I stand on the line, a feat (no pun intended) that significantly shortens your casting range. Outdoors, the situation is far worse. There are an infinite variety of obstacles, living and dead, large and small, that stand ever alert to snag a fly line that has fallen its way. Over the years, broken clamshells, seaweed, twigs, rocks, pebbles, cats, and even fiddler crabs have fouled my fly line and ruined my casts. Similar to Murphy's Law, the rule is, if there is anything that can possibly catch or snare a fly line, you can bet that inevitably it will do so.

Boat decks are a good example. Today, most boats designated as "fishing machines" are generally not designed expressly for fly-fishing and you'll have to take extra measures to see to it that obstacles are minimized. For example, if the boat cleats are not the type that recess into the gunwale, they will have to be taped over or covered with tubing so they won't catch the line. As I mentioned in the previous chapter, even specially designed fly-fishing boats like the ones with flush casting decks can pose a problem because if it gets windy (it's a rare day when it doesn't), the line laying on the deck will be blown into the water. This is bad enough if the boat is staked out or anchored, but if it's drifting, which is usually the case, line trailing behind in the water will cause some monumental hassles. I lost my chance for a trophy-size striper on a flat off Martha's Vineyard because the fly line was blown off the deck and I couldn't recover it in time to make the cast. Adding insult to injury was the fact that my stripping basket was sitting right beside the console. I didn't think I needed it while casting from the pristine platform of Captain Jaime Boyles' super flats skiff. All it took was one brief gust of wind to prove me wrong.

Step off a boat and the conditions can be far more challenging. The rough surface normally found on beaches, rocks, jetties and breakwaters can really chew up a fly line as well as tangle or foul the line during the cast. Wading into the water can be worse yet. Especially in the surf, the water turbulence alone will cause you endless tangles and snarls if you simply allow the line to fall into the water. Even in much calmer conditions like a shallow-water tidal flat, line lying on the water will impede its castability. The surface of the water acts like a magnet attaching itself to the fly line so even a floating line cannot be lifted as easily as would be the case if it were lying on a flat, relatively dry platform. You will find that this added resistance can shorten your casts by as much as 15 to 18 feet.

A stripping basket will not only protect the fly line from costly snags and tangles, it will also make it possible for two anglers to simultaneously share a boat's casting platform. Normally if two anglers on a boat wish to fly-fish at the same time, one will have to cast from the bow, the other from the stern. This can be a dicey game if both are right-handed casters and want to fish the same side of the boat. Unless one angler makes back-handed casts, one caster will always be throwing a line to the left side of the other person. But if both are using a basket, each can safely cast standing side by side. All they have to do is alternate positions after completing their cast.

John Posh and I did this repeatedly on a bonefishing trip in Honduras. Both of us stood on the casting deck. Either John or I would make the first cast and immediately switch sides so the other person could make their presentation. There were no problems with either of us standing on the other's line and because the casts were only a few seconds apart, we were able to get a number of double hookups from the same school of fish.

Bob Popovics, Ed Jaworowski and myself carried this one step further fishing Cape Cod one summer with Captain Dan Marini. All of us were wearing our stripping baskets. One of us would fish in the stern and execute the forward cast by turning sideways and making a backhand stroke with the right hand to deliver the fly. That way the line didn't come across the boat. It sailed safely behind the outboard engine. The other two would share the bow, switching sides and alternating their casts.

Dan liked the idea because with three flies hitting the water in quick succession, each spot he took us to was thoroughly covered. As an added bonus, if bass were concentrated in a certain area, it wasn't uncommon to have two or three hookups going at the same time. None of this would have been possible without stripping baskets to contain the line. The frequent changes in the boat's drifting pattern coupled with intermittent shifts in

A stripping basket is an invaluable tool anywhere you wade.

wind direction would have blown our lines all over the place making it impossible to get off clean casts.

There are baskets commercially available from a number of sources. You can purchase them from large companies like Orvis. If you live in the Northeast there are a number of tackle and specialty fly shops that sell baskets custom made by some of the locals. The rigid types are usually made from some form of plastic and they tend to do a better job of storing the line than the mesh type baskets. The mesh sides are prone to collapsing in on themselves and this can cause the line to tangle. This won't happen with the rigid models but some anglers are reluctant to pack them along on trips because they feel they will take up too much room in their luggage. However, if you are using the soft-type luggage as most anglers are doing

nowadays, it's not a problem to pack a rigid basket in one of the bags. Once inside the bag, you can stuff the basket will all kinds of things from clothes to tackle items. And because the basket is both rigid and flexible, it will actually provide an added measure of protection for the items you place in it.

Be advised, however, that there is no one basket that is ideal for all conditions you are likely to encounter. But since they are inexpensive and easy to make, it's not a problem to have several different types. For fishing the surf I prefer a deep plastic container. The ones intended for use as wastepaper baskets work fine. One of my favorites that I've been using for almost 30 years is a simple, rectangular container that is approximately 15 inches deep and 7 inches wide. The flat sides fit snugly against my hip and the added depth prevents line from spilling out in the event I have to run down the beach to reach breaking fish. Especially in an environment like the high surf, you can expect water to splash in from pounding waves so it's a good idea to punch holes in the bottom of the basket to facilitate quick draining. To secure the basket around my waist, I make two holes near the corners of the wide side where I can secure the hooks from a length of bungee cord. With this arrangement, I can move the basket around to my rear when I'm fighting a fish, or if need be, I can get rid of it quickly by simply undoing the hook from the hole.

When fishing from a boat or wading calmer waters like a bay, estuary or tidal flat, a stripping basket made from a dishpan-like container is a better choice. One particular container I especially like is a storage basket marketed as Stuff and Tote. It measures 10 x 14 1/2 x 16 inches. To help prevent line from fouling in the basket, a variety of contrivances have been inserted into the bottom of the container ranging from indoor-outdoor carpeting to cone-shaped projections. Taking a cue from Ed Jaworowski who has seriously studied the matter, I've found that a series of flexible monofilament spikes is the best arrangement for minimizing line tangles. The key here is flexibility. If the monofilament strands bend as line is shooting up out of the basket, there is less likelihood that the coils will interlock or foul. I know a number of anglers who have given up on shooting heads because of the frequent tangles they would experience with the small-diameter shooting lines. But with the flexible spike arrangement, I've found that even when fishing with 80 to 100 feet of monofilament running line in the basket, the fouling problem seldom occurs.

The mono spikes can be fashioned from any number of brand-name monofilaments. You just have to bear in

Kayaks have become popular water craft among fly-fishers.

worth it when you consider all the mishaps you suffer when your line falls haphazardly whenever you happen to be standing. While it may not be wise to put all your eggs in one basket, it's certainly a good practice where fly lines are concerned.

Water Craft

Fishing afoot affords a unique blend of challenge and excitement and there are many accomplished anglers who prefer this as their principle means of fishing. However, there are inherent limitations with the foot-leg express so when the opportunity presents itself, inevitably even the most ardent shore-bound angler will hop into some type of water craft to better pursue his quarry. These may range from float tubes to multi-million-dollar mega yachts. With the exception of a yacht class vessel which I could never afford to purchase or maintain, over the years I've owned, operated and fished from all manner of contrivances designed to carry you to where the fish are. Each had their limitations and fine points—some I swore at, others I swore by, but I caught fish from all of them.

My earliest experiences were in wooden rowboats with my uncles who took me fishing in Long Island Sound. Old salts refer to the oar-based propulsion of these boats as the "ash breeze" and every time I climb into one I have fond memories of my youth. In those days no one I was affiliated with could afford an outboard motor, but in lieu of fitness centers and home exercise equipment, rowing proved a great way to stay in shape. The principle bonus of course was that it enabled you to fish, and though we didn't realize it at the time, the stealth-like approach afforded by oars often proved more effective than the noisy intrusion of the early generation outboards we all coveted.

When I moved to Southern California with my family, I continued the tradition and saved enough money from mowing lawns and waxing cars to buy an old wooden skiff with two friends. It had a hole in the bottom that you could easily pass a bowling ball through, but with the help of a local commercial fisherman, we got it patched. The first Saturday following the repair job we headed out to Redondo Canyon, a very deep trench in the ocean bottom that was only a mile or so from shore.

mind that for any given pound test the diameter and stiffness of monofilament line will differ according to the particular manufacturer. Generally lines in the 80- to 150-pound-test range will do the job. When sold as leader material, some line is already pre-straightened. If it's in coils, you have to straighten it yourself. Cut the line in one-foot lengths and place it in a tube that can be capped to hold water. I use nickel diameter PVC tubing. Boil some water and then pour it into the tube. Allow it to sit for about five minutes, pour it out and then fill the tube with cold water. After a few minutes time the line should be straight. Depending on the dimensions of the basket, anywhere from 15 to 25 stands of mono 5 to 7 inches in length can be glued to the bottom of the container. It's best to pre-drill holes in the bottom of the basket with a drill bit approximately the same diameter as the mono spikes. Push the spikes up through the holes. Then using a heated knife blade, flatten the bottom end of the spikes to prevent them from slipping back through the holes. Then glue the flattened ends to the bottom of the container with a non-water soluble glue. One I like to use is Marine Tex.

The one major complaint about stripping baskets seems to be from people who are not accustomed to wearing one, they say they're uncomfortable or that the basket impedes their stripping motion. The simple remedy for this is continued use. It will take a little time and patience to get used to a basket. But with practice comes familiarity and eventually wearing a basket will be as natural as donning a fishing vest (actually I'm more comfortable with a basket). The little effort it takes to get accustomed to wearing and using a basket is well

School size bluefin tuna used to cruise this area but since we didn't have any live bait or means of containing them, we settled for the bonito that went for our feathered jigs. Everything went fine until we started to head back in. The year was 1957 and the King Harbor breakwater was nearing completion. Rowing sideways to the strong current, we cut the entrance to the harbor too close. We tried to reposition ourselves but it was too late. I saw the large swell coming so my friend and I shipped the oars, grabbed the edges of the bench seat and hung on for a ride that proved to be a lot more thrilling than anything we experienced at the local amusement parks. The wave lifted us so high that I could see the end of the parking lot. I remember for a brief second wishing I was one of the onlookers standing there watching this unfold instead of being the one who was about to get pummeled. True to the gravitational principle that tells us whatever goes up must come down, the next sensory input that dominated my mind was the sound of the boat bottom being punctured by the partially submerged boulders. I've never heard a noise quite like that again and I hope I never do. Reflecting back on this, it's amazing that the 16-foot skiff actually made it over the rocks and that none of us were hurt. However, the bottom was almost completely torn out and we lost most of our hard-earned fishing tackle. With the exception of a couple of trips on the party boats, we had to make do with surf fishing the entire summer.

In 1970 when I left California to take an assistant professor position at the City University of New York, I rewarded myself with the purchase of a new, Ray Hunt designed, 22-foot center-console boat manufactured by a company called Highliner in New Hampshire. Like so many boat companies, they've come and gone, but this was a worthy vessel and I learned a great deal about boating. At least one lesson that did not come the hard way was the fact that choosing the right boat involves compromises, probably more so than any other major purchase you're likely to undertake. At least I knew my intended purpose for the boat. I didn't want it for water skiing, racing, cruising or family picnics. I wanted it for fishing. More specifically, I wanted it for stand-up, light-tackle and fly-fishing. While these specifications do narrow your range of options, there are numerous considerations that still have to be factored in. Of paramount concern here is the species on which you intend to focus. What you fish for has a great deal to do with the type of conditions you can expect to encounter with your boat. If there are just a few species that you wish to target and they happen to frequent the same type of water, your choices are easier. For example, if you are interested primarily in tuna and billfish, you can limit your boat choices to those craft that are designed for offshore fishing. On the other hand, if bonefish and redfish are your passion, you should be looking at shallow draft boats designed to run in skinny water. Unfortunately for many people, things aren't that simple. If you like to fish for a variety of species that inhabit different locales, you can have some difficult decisions in choosing a boat that will best suit your needs.

When I bought my first center console, I intended to fish primarily for striped bass and bluefish. That presented a bit of a problem because these two species can be found in very different kinds of water. I decided to dock the boat at a particular locale in Long Island Sound. It was in Cos Cob, Connecticut. But the fact that blues invade the rock-laden shallows as well as deep-water spots in the middle of the sound, posed a problem regarding the type of boat I should buy. Do you settle on one that has a shallow draft intended for inshore use, or should you go to a deep V-hull configuration that is better suited for big-water conditions? Actually my choices at the time were more limited simply because there were fewer boats from which to choose. I had fished off flats skiffs in Florida, but at the time no one was using these in the Northeast and I never considered them for the type of fishing I would be doing. I settled on the Ray Hunt designed deep V and was very happy with it, but it still represented a compromise. The boat was at its best when I fished in deep water or made long runs across the sound. It had its limitations in shallow water, something that I learned to accept after wiping out a few costly props on the rocks.

Today, in the Northeast, flats boats have become extremely popular among fly-fishers and guides. If you are going to concentrate on the flats, that's fine. But if you constantly have to run in open deep water where there is likely to be large swells or a steep chop, you have to recognize that you'll be better served with a type of boat that has a deeper V hull and considerably more free-board. Not too long ago, fishing off Montauk in a flats skiff almost proved disastrous. There was nothing wrong with the boat, it was a top-name skiff from a well-respected manufacturer, but it wasn't suitable for the conditions we were up against. We were only about 30 yards from the rock-studded shore, but the wind and current were working in opposite directions and the result was some downright nasty water. It was so rough that I had to make my casts from a sitting position on the seat in front of the console. I couldn't stand and strip line because I needed one hand to hang onto the console grab rail. The guide was keeping an eye out for the surf and after each of my casting-and-retrieving sequences, he would reposition us further back from the breaking waves. But despite all his caution, he still couldn't prevent us from getting swamped. I was just about to shoot a cast into the frothing white foam churning behind a large boulder, when I heard him yell, "hang on." Suddenly I felt the icy sensation of cold water running down my neck and back. I was hunched over staring down at the deck and could see water swirling around my ankles. Fly boxes, tippet spools, hand towels and various clothing items were sloshing all around me. For some reason, instead of being seized by the danger of the moment, the first image that came to mind was one of those plastic kiddy pools filled with all sorts of floating toys. Fortunately the batteries were secured in watertight boxes and the big Yamaha outboard kept running. As testimony to the quality of the boat and engine, the guide quickly had us turned around and making headway and the water gradually drained back into the sea. We were now out of danger, but the ride back to the dock was the wettest I ever experienced. I literally felt like I was being sprayed by a high-pressure hose. The boat, along with my back and rear end, also took a terrific pounding.

This is not to imply that you're destined for disaster if you start running a flats skiff offshore. As with any boat, you have to be aware of their inherent limitations and keep a sharp weather eye. My friend Corbett Davis, Jr. has a 17-foot Maverick that he routinely uses to fish the protected waters in Pensacola Bay. But he also tows it to Mobile, Alabama where he fishes the offshore oil platforms. I've had some great trips out there with him when we ran up behind shrimp boats culling their catch.

Returning to Southern California in the early seventies, I quickly became disenchanted with the prospect of trying to fly-fish from the party boats. I needed to have my own boat once again, and this time the choice was considerably easier. In Southern California there is no shallow-water fishing akin to what you find in places like the Gulf, the Keys and parts of the Northeast where there are extensive tidal flats. Even inshore, in most places including the bays and harbors, the water is fairly deep. Off the coast it's all open ocean. If you miss Catalina or San Clemente Island, next stop is Hawaii. I talked to Lefty about the kinds of conditions I would be facing and he told me in no uncertain terms that there was a boat that was tailor made for the type of water in which I would be running. As so many boats are today,

it was made in Florida. The boat was a SeaCraft and there was only one dealer in Southern California. I went to him, took a test ride in the 20-footer and asked him to start the paperwork as soon as we got back to the dock. If I had the money, I would have opted for the larger 23-footer, but when you add just a couple of feet to a boat, the price escalates almost exponentially. At the minimum, you'll need a bigger motor. That translates into higher fuel bills. Larger trailers (don't forget the towing vehicle) and increased dockage fees are also part of the package. When I look back on it, the 20-footer was really all the boat I needed. There were many times when I ran over 50 miles offshore and the SeaCraft never let me down.

Now more than 30 years later, in addition to the established companies there are a number of new manufacturers who are making some excellent boats. So even if you are sure about the type of boat that will best suit your needs, the availability of all these fine craft can make the selection process very difficult. I have friends, some of whom are guides, who fish various parts of the country in boats that run the full spectrum of what the industry currently has to offer. They fish practically every conceivable type of water and their boat choices are as varied as the conditions they face. Conway Bowman whose specializes in sharks off San Diego loves his 18-foot Parker. A little further north, Bill Matthews is equally fond of his 20-foot Hydra-Sports. Jimbo Meador fishes the shallows around Mobile, Alabama and swears by his skiff from Hell's Bay Boatworks. Corbett is partial to his Maverick. Scott Paciello just bought a Regulator for his home waters around Staten Island, Joe Keegan charters out of northeast Connecticut with a SeaCat catamaran and Ernie French had Steiger Craft modify their 21-foot skiff for his guiding work off the east end of Long Island. These are all great boats and every one of these knowledgeable anglers feels they made the right choice for their particular needs. However, they will all concede that each of their vessels represents a tradeoff. To emphasize some features, you sacrifice others. It's a fact of life in the boating world.

A far cry from the boats I've owned is my experience with float tubes in the ocean. The fact that I no longer do this says something about how I feel about it. Harry Kime's experience in Baja that I referred to in the last chapter always seemed to occupy my thoughts every time I drifted around in one in the ocean. I never felt at ease. One time off the Palos Verdes peninsula about 15 miles south of Los Angeles International Airport, I was working my way alongside a kelp bed when I saw a large,

Captain Gene Quigley's fly-fishing machine, a 21-foot Parker Special Edition.

my rod and reel in one hand and an underwater camera strapped around my neck. When I finally reached the surf line, I took one hell of a pounding and lost an expensive pair of prescription polarized glasses that I forget to secure in one of the canvass pockets.

From the float tube I graduated to an ocean kayak. It was much more mobile and secure than the tube, but I still suffered my share of mishaps. Mine was an open model that you sat on top of much like a paddleboard. That made it virtually unsinkable, which was a godsend considering how many

dark profile heading my way. Did you ever try to climb out of a float tube in the water? It can't be done. Fortunately, the ominous shape proved to be that of a large seal that apparently was curious about this strange object bobbing along in its home waters.

My next trip out after that was my last. I had a very productive morning catching nice size calico bass on fly. Even if you don't always subscribe to a policy of catch and release, it's something you should definitely adhere to if you're dangling from a float tube in the ocean. I always made it a practice to do so. Similar to their fresh-water cousins, calicos do not have teeth designed to puncture or tear, making it possible to lip them with your bare fingers. I did this with numerous bass I caught that morning, but in maneuvering them to within reach, the sharp spines from their dorsal fins pierced the float tube. I was preoccupied with the unnerving thought of a shark cruising by intent on devouring what I was trying to quickly relinquish so quite some time elapsed before I realized what was happening. My first clue was a curious hissing sound. At first I thought it might have been some bug buzzing around the kelp bed. I continued to fish and noticed that my back casts began striking the surface with all too frequent regularity. I finally realized that I was sitting lower to the surface. The float tube was deflating. I wasn't afraid of drowning because I was wearing a full wet suit with skin-diver type fins. But it was very difficult to effect forward movement. The combination of the flat tube with its canvass covering made for considerable dead weight. I was further hampered with

times I tipped over. There is a similar model now being offered by Cobra Kayaks called the Fish N Dive. It has a wider beam than my old kayak which gives it more stability. It also has an incredible 600-pound carrying capacity. Two other kayaks worth considering are the Tribalance and the Stealth. The Tribalance has two adaptable outriggers that afford amazing stability. In calm water you can even stand up in it. The Stealth from Kiwikayak has a double hull which also makes it practically impossible to tip over.

Aside from common sense and safety precautions, I also do not recommend going out or coming in where there are high-surf conditions. This takes practice and you'll have to be prepared for numerous wipeouts before you become proficient at it. With their stealth-like silence, kayaks can be very efficient in protected shallow waters and on the flats. About their only limitation, is the limited ability to sight fish as a result of their extremely low profile in the water. If you have easy access points, they make for a very economical and efficient alternative to a flats skiff.

Whatever type of watercraft you choose—from kayaks to car top skiffs to large ocean-going vessels—it's vitally important that you learn the rudiments of navigation. There are no highways on the water and much more so than land-based locales, the marine environment is a wide-open, ever-changing world. Aside from the water itself, which can present a host of challenges in the form of waves and currents, beneath the surface there are all kinds of hidden dangers like rocks, reefs, wrecks and sand bars. Some have signposts

A Baja roosterfish.

alerting you to their presence but they are useless unless you understand what they mean. Many other potential hazards are unmarked save for notations on nautical charts. The chart is a nautical road map, but it can't alert you to dangerous routes if you don't know how to read it. To safely traverse a course to and from your destination, you should be familiar with the basic tools of navigation, comprised of a compass, chart and depth-finding equipment.

Obviously you may not need all these tools every time you're out on the water, but at the minimum, even in a float tube or kayak, I would at least carry a compass and know how to use it. When you're on the water, perspectives change. What were once familiar landmarks look different from the water, and gauging distances can be a lot more deceiving. Even with good visibility, it can be difficult to judge your exact position. If you can't see your way, things can get real scary. I'm not just thinking about nightfall. Anywhere you have a body of water, there is the possibility of thick, blinding fog and you can get in serious trouble if you don't know where you are or where you should be going.

One early spring when I fishing with a friend from his skiff in Long Beach Harbor, a thick fog started blowing in from seaward and he quickly took some bearings and established our position. In a matter of minutes we were completely enveloped and I could barely make out his profile which wasn't more than 15 feet from where I was standing in the bow. Earlier that afternoon, we spotted three people in float tubes but didn't pay much attention to them aside from commenting to one another that we thought they were crazy for being out here in those floating donuts. Since we knew where we were and the bite was still pretty good with sand bass, rather than running in the soup, we decided to drop anchor and continue fishing. In the fog it can be difficult to establish the true direction of sound, but we heard guys yelling to one another and judging by the sound of one guy's voice, he was close to panic. We yelled back and established contact. It was the trio in the float tubes and they had no clue as to their position or where they were heading. Gradually by shouting back and forth we got them heading in our direction. Judging by our compass bearing, if they continued their original course, they would have found themselves at the entrance to the harbor. This is not a good place to be in a float-tube. The currents can be real strong and on an outgoing tide you can be easily swept outside the breakwater. In addition, boats crossing the harbor entrance (particularly the large tankers) might not spot a float tube on their radar and this could make for a real tragedy. If the float-tube boys had a hand-held compass, they could have figured an approximate course back to the launch ramp which would have put them in a lot safer water compared to where they were heading.

Even if you aren't the owner or principal operator of the craft, if you plan to spend much time on the water, I strongly recommend taking a boating course to learn the fundamentals of piloting and seamanship. The United States Power Squadron and the Coast Guard Auxiliary both offer such courses to the general public. What you learn will not only make you safer on the water, it will also help you be a more successful angler.

Fishing is my life, it's my world, it's my consuming passion. I'm sure that most of you who have picked up this book feel much the same way. But like it or not, the hard reality is that if we want to continue to enjoy this both for ourselves and for those who come after us, we have to fight to preserve the resource.

A Word on Conservation

Back in 1980 I was asked to sit as the sportfishing representative on the Pacific Fishery Management Council. I was very surprised at the appointment because I wasn't politically connected or particularly politically active. As I was to learn to later on, the appointment was initiated by an aide to California governor Jerry Brown who I met on a fishing trip in Baja. My friends congratulated me but there were others in the sportfishing industry who were plain jealous of my appointment. That's a sad commentary on the recreational fishery, but unfortunately it's often been the case where people get involved in various conservation efforts primarily as a means of enhancing their own egos. As sport fishermen we don't need that. Preserving the resource is a stand-up political slug match and I agree with Lefty and others who argue that we need paid professional lobbyists who know their way around the state capitals and Washington to don the gloves for us.

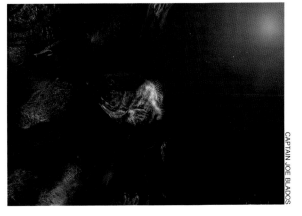

CAPTAIN JOE BLADOS

I took my appointment very seriously, but as one vote out of thirteen, I was truly the lone voice in the wilderness. The commercial interests were well organized and well represented. In stark contrast, I was always playing a game of catch up. Fishery data that was timely and unbiased was difficult for me to come by but not for the commercial boys. They had a paid staff that did all their homework. To make matters worse, there were even times when I learned that information was deliberately withheld from me simply because some bruised egos wanted to be on center stage. The commercial sector knows better. They're not about to let personalities stand in the way of furthering their interests.

I think we've come a long way since then, but this is the kind of struggle where you can't relax because the commercial interests will always try and maximize their harvest. This is not to cast commercial fishermen as bad guys. There are many who want to see the resource preserved because it is their livelihood and they genuinely like to fish for a living. But history is living testimony to the fact that too many times the overwhelming desire to make a buck has resulted in management decisions and quota allocations that have been disastrous for the fishery. I didn't believe it at the time, but after three years of sitting on the Council, I'm convinced that there are people out there who don't give a damn about the future of any resource. These are the types who would cut down the last remaining redwood or take the very last salmon and then go on to something else. They feel it's their right to exploit a resource for profit and as long as it can be harvested, they will try and do so irrespective of the consequences.

So what are we to do as recreational fishermen? Well, aside from practicing good conservation measures ourselves, which means that we should put back most of what we catch, we should support organized groups that will fight to preserve what we love to do. Unless you are a physician or a lawyer, you usually do not attempt to solve your own medical or legal problems. Instead, you rely on qualified experts and I think the same strategy applies when facing fishery issues. Give your support to the conservation efforts of organizations like the International Game Fish Association and the United Federation of Anglers Conservation Foundation. You may recall that famous cry from the pages of American history, "United we stand, divided we fall." Effective organization was critical to the development of this country. Likewise, it's also vital for the preservation of our fisheries. It is my hope that generations after us will continue to experience the thrill of tight lines, bent rods and strong-pulling fish.

Product Info

Products For Saltwater Fly-Fishers

Any time product sources are listed there are two potential shortfalls. For one, the particular item may no longer be available. Secondly, manufacturers not mentioned may feel slighted. I am mindful of these risks but in the interest of providing what I hope will serve as a useful information source, I offer the following abbreviated list of products directed at the saltwater fly-fisher. If I were limited to just one source, it would be Bob Marriott's Annual Guide to Fly-Fishing. Products that will serve virtually all your fly-fishing needs can be found in this comprehensive catalogue. If you can't visit the store, this is the next best bet.

Bob Marriott's
www.bobmarriotts.com, 1•800•535•6633.

AirFlo fly lines
info@mainstreamusa.com, 1•800•672•6866

Rio fly lines
www.rioproducts.com, 208•524•7760

Scientific Anglers
www.scientificanglers.com

Sufix monofilament line
1•800•554•1423

Powell fly rods
www.powellco.com, 916•852•2150

Redington fly rods
www.redington.com, 1•800•253•2538

St. Croix fly rods
www.stcroixrods.com, 1•800•826•7042

Scott fly rods
www.scottflyrod.com, 970•249•3180

Sage fly rods
www.sageflyfish.com, 1•800•533•3004

Thomas and Thomas fly rods
www.thomasandthomas.com,
413•863•9727

Abel fly reels
www.abelreels.com, 805•826•7042

Islander fly reels
www.islander.com, 250•544•1440

Tibor fly reels
www.tiborreel.com, 561•272•0770

Enrico Puglisi Flies
www.epflies.com

Umpqua Flies
www.umpqua.com, 1•800•322•3218

Renzetti fly-tying vises
www.renzetti.com, 321•267•7705

Mustad hooks
www.mustad.no

Gamakatsu hooks
253•922•8373

Varivas hooks
201•451•6272

Simms wading apparel
www.simmsfishing.com, 406•585•3557